Praise for
Nine Common Lies Christians Believe

"Do you cringe when hearing another Christian cliché? Are you weary of how unhelpful (and unbiblical) some of our Christian vernacular has become? In this book my friend Shane Pruitt addresses some of the statements that have run amuck in our midst and have inevitably weakened the voice of the church in our culture. I highly recommend you read this book and discuss it with a group of friends."

—ED STETZER, Billy Graham distinguished chair
at Wheaton College

"Shane's book will help all of us understand the true character of God in a deeper way and be ready to encourage friends and family who have fallen prey to these common lies."

—SCOTT EVANS, founder and president of Outreach Inc.

"It's the book we all need to read. It's the book we need to encourage others to read. It's the book about lies we have heard and maybe even believed throughout our Christian lives. Shane Pruitt takes the lies and turns them upside down to point us to biblical truth. He writes from the heart of one who loves Scripture but also from the heart of one who has had to endure these lies amid his own heartaches in his family. Thank you, Shane. *Nine Common Lies Christians Believe* is a gift to all of us."

—THOM RAINER, president and CEO of LifeWay Christian
Resources Church Answers, ChurchAnswers.com

"Shane's book encompasses my two favorite themes: the restorative grace of Jesus Christ and adoption. This book is sure to encourage you!"

—Lisa Sharon Harper, speaker and author of *The Sacrament of Happy*

"The evangelical world has been waiting to hear from a fresh young voice like Shane Pruitt. He has a passion for people and a love for the Lord and is straight as an arrow theologically. Read this new book . . . and reap!"

—O. S. Hawkins, president and CEO of GuideStone Financial Resources and best-selling author of *The Joshua Code*

"Finally! I am so thankful that Shane has addressed these lies so winsomely and pointed us toward the real truth of God's Word! This book will be a tremendous encouragement to people going through a difficult time, wanting to know God's Word better, or simply looking to increase their faith. I urge you to read it and share it with everyone you know!"

—Jonathan "JP" Pokluda, teaching pastor at Watermark Community Church, leader of The Porch, and author of *Welcome to Adulting*

"I've been in church my entire life and had no idea that some of the clichés that are often regurgitated aren't at all biblical. In *Nine Common Lies Christians Believe*, Shane Pruitt articulately lays out a biblically sound doctrine that is both convicting and a breath of fresh air!"

—LAWRENCE B. JONES III, news contributor for Fox News, CNN, and MSNBC and editor in chief of Campus Reform

"Here's a clear and compelling antidote to the kind of common clichés that so many people uncritically believe. Thanks, Shane, for pointing readers to biblical wisdom, where hope and truth reside!"

—LEE STROBEL, *New York Times* best-selling author of *The Case for Christ* and *The Case for Faith*

"Without consistent discipleship, Christians can fall prey to lies they've heard regularly in the church. In *Nine Common Lies Christians Believe*, Shane successfully navigates some of the most common false beliefs told in the church. By speaking the truth in love, he firmly and gracefully provides a much-needed course correction. Every Christian will benefit from reading this book."

—ROBBY GALLATY, senior pastor at Long Hollow Baptist Church and author of *Growing Up* and *The Forgotten Jesus*

"Like Paul Laurence Dunbar's "We Wear the Mask," Shane Pruitt's *Nine Common Lies Christians Believe* allows us to collectively exhale, exposing humanity's propensity to hide. Unlike

Dunbar's poem, Shane's prose welcomes us into the land of vulnerability, embraced by a Father who loves us."

—BRYAN LORITTS, lead pastor at Abundant Life Church
and author of *Insider Outsider*

"Jesus never said that following Him was going to be easy. When Christians reduce faith to pithy statements like the lies Shane breaks down in this book, it doesn't help—it actually hurts. So stop believing these lies! Let my friend Shane guide and lead you to understanding the heart of God."

—DANIEL IM, teaching pastor at The Fellowship, director
of church multiplication at LifeWay Christian Resources,
podcaster, and author of *No Silver Bullets*

"In my time in ministry, I can't tell you how often I've heard Christians articulate some version of each of the statements in this book. I'm so glad Shane wrote this book, addressing these lies from a biblical perspective. Shane Pruitt is a voice we need to hear more from."

—MATT CARTER, pastor of preaching and vision at
The Austin Stone Community Church and author
of *Steal Away Home*

9 COMMON LIES CHRISTIANS BELIEVE

9 COMMON LIES CHRISTIANS BELIEVE

AND WHY GOD'S TRUTH IS INFINITELY BETTER

SHANE PRUITT

MULTNOMAH

NINE COMMON LIES CHRISTIANS BELIEVE

All Scripture quotations are taken from the Holy Bible, English Standard Version, ESV®
Text Edition® (2016), copyright © 2001 by Crossway Bibles, a publishing ministry of
Good News Publishers. All rights reserved.

Trade Paperback ISBN 978-0-7352-9157-7
eBook ISBN 978-0-7352-9158-4

Copyright © 2019 by Michael Shane Pruitt

Cover design by Kristopher K. Orr

All rights reserved. No part of this book may be reproduced or transmitted in any form or
by any means, electronic or mechanical, including photocopying and recording, or by any
information storage and retrieval system, without permission in writing from the publisher.

Published in the United States by Multnomah, an imprint of the Crown Publishing
Group, a division of Penguin Random House LLC, New York.

MULTNOMAH® and its mountain colophon are registered trademarks of Penguin Random
House LLC.

The Cataloging-in-Publication Data is on file with the Library of Congress.

Printed in the United States of America
2019—First Edition

10 9 8 7 6 5 4 3 2 1

SPECIAL SALES
Most Multnomah books are available at special quantity discounts when purchased in
bulk by corporations, organizations, and special-interest groups. Custom imprinting
or excerpting can also be done to fit special needs. For information, please email
specialmarketscms@penguinrandomhouse.com or call 1-800-603-7051.

This book is dedicated to the love of my life, Kasi. Also to our children, Raygen, Harper, Titus, Elliot, and Glory. Getting to take this journey called life with you is an absolute joy and privilege. May we always walk in God's truth.

Oh, magnify the Lord with me,
and let us exalt his name together!

—Psalm 34:3

Contents

The Truth Shall Set You Free from Bad One-Liners

One one-thousand. Two one-thousand. Three one-thousand. Deep breath. Keep it in. Just breathe . . . It took every ounce of will-power within me to suppress the urge to scream at the top of my voice. But with God as my witness, I never uttered a word. Instead, if you could have seen the thought bubble above my head, well, let's just say it wasn't one of my most spiritual moments. Yes, rather than completely freaking out my neighbors who were out-side at the time, I bit my tongue (almost off) and set my sights on an orange flowerpot and viciously spiked it into the ground like a football. That helped, a little. No, not really.

Here I was, a church planter and pastor of a rapidly growing congregation. My wife and I were happily married. We lived in a multiple-bedroom house. We had friends and family surrounding us with love and encouragement. Yet I was standing in the backyard, screaming in my head and spiking flowerpots with my hands. In case you don't know, here's the deal. We pastors consistently feel extreme pressure to mask our weaknesses. We don't have the freedom to be ticked off. We must always keep it classy and cheesy with an arsenal of Christian clichés at our disposal. On the outside, we love for you to believe we're walking in the freedom of truth, but on the inside, we know it's fake. Sadly, we're too good at selling the fake, and we're trapped by common lies that we believe all too quickly. Or at least I was.

One of my neighbors gave me a puzzled look. "Shane, you all right, brother?"

Almost without thinking, I said, "Absolutely! You know me. I'm too blessed to be stressed, my man!"

I cannot believe I really said that. The truth is, it was a lie! I was broken, confused, and flat out sick and tired of hearing one-liners wrapped in pretty Christian paper but offering no power to help us in what we were going through as a family.

And what were we dealing with? All right, sure, I'll tell you.

As a couple, Kasi and I always knew we wanted to adopt. It was something we talked about from the minute we got married. We planned on having biological children first and then starting the adoption process. We had it all figured out, or so we thought. After we'd had two daughters, both of us had a picture in our minds of what our son would be like. We envisioned him playing with our girls, excelling in football, and growing healthy and strong. Needless to say, we imagined *The Blind Side* version of adoption. However, our creative God had a plan to put to death our shallow view of the picture-perfect family.

When we began the process to adopt, our two biological daughters were six years and eight months old. Kasi and I had no idea what this journey would entail, but we knew without a doubt that God was calling us to adoption in this particular season of our lives. We started researching agencies, found one, and began praying through the countries the agency worked with. Initially, we decided to pray about it for several days, but that first night, we had a feeling of peace that Uganda was the place we'd find our son. We did all the paperwork and training, and then the real wait started. We were on a waiting list and soon found out it would most likely take much longer than we'd ever imagined. So we waited and prayed for the son we knew was there but had never met. Ironically, Kasi would often pray that God would bring us a child no one else wanted—a child who needed love and a family but had little to no hope of either. Still, we both visualized what our son would be—big, muscular, and Christmas card photo ready.

Kasi woke up one morning and discovered an email from someone she knew only through Facebook. The person asked if we were open to adopting a child with special needs. Kasi wrote back asking for some clarification. We knew very little about special needs but enough to understand it is a very, very broad term. Special needs could describe something as small as a missing finger or as big as needing constant in-depth care. Kasi found out the little boy in question had gangrene and needed surgery as soon as possible. After she shared the email with me, we both decided to take the next step of finding out more.

Soon we received an email from the director of the children's home, telling us more about him. This baby, named Praise, was severely malnourished and had a huge infection on his head. And then we saw his picture. Tiny. Precious. We fell in love immediately. Could this be our hoped-for son?

We asked for as much medical information as possible. What followed was a picture we'll never forget. On the first picture we received, his infection had been covered. Not on this one. When we viewed this picture, our stomachs dropped. We could hardly speak, and Kasi began weeping.

We prayed, hugged, prayed, cried, and prayed more. It was as if we both knew what God was clearly telling us to do, even though we initially didn't want to admit it. We struggled with thoughts like *We can't handle this. This is going to be too hard. We have no clue what we're doing, what he needs, or how to take care of him. We certainly don't have time to take on something like this.*

After much information and even more prayer, we decided this sweet, tiny boy was indeed our son, the one we had been praying for all along. *Okay! We can handle this after all,* we thought. *We're ministry leaders, which means we have a huge S on our chests for being Super Christians, right?*

Kasi and I traveled to Uganda to complete the legal process to adopt. When we met our son, whom we named Titus, we could tell he was developmentally delayed, but we attributed this to his being in the hospital his entire life. As time went by, we began to sense something more going on than we were initially told.

Upon our return, Kasi made an appointment for us to see an

international adoption doctor. One of the things we'd noticed in Uganda was that our son was very stiff. He also had some spells of jumping and jerking. We explained all this to the doctor, and he admitted Titus for observation. What was initially supposed to be one night turned into four. During this stay, we learned that there was much more going on with our son and that our suspicions were correct.

The short version is that Titus was experiencing seizures—a lot of seizures. At the time, he was having over twenty a day. He also had some trauma to his brain, and it wasn't quite the size it should be for a seven-month-old boy. The doctors couldn't give us any clear picture of what his life would be like. Would he catch up? Would he walk? Would he talk? These were answers we desperately wanted, but they were answers the doctors couldn't provide.

One day his doctors came into the hospital room, shut the door, turned off the television, and said they needed to talk. That day our life changed forever. We sat in shock while our son was diagnosed with epilepsy and cerebral palsy. Most likely, he'll always be in a wheelchair, we won't ever get to play catch with him or see him run up and down a hill, and we'll never be empty nesters.

Lord, what are You doing? This is not what we asked for, nor is this what we agreed to. Right, God? We had an agreement. After all, we're doing something spiritual here. We're caring for orphans like You commanded! This was Your idea! We're being obedient, unlike other "superficial" Christians. Come on, God, we're probably Your favorite pastor and pastor's wife, so You should honor our wishes and our good and perfect plan for our lives! We can't handle this!

A Most Dangerous Game

Over the next year of constant doctor's appointments, an MRI, an EEG, and three surgeries, we fell into a routine, almost a kind of game. It was a game of convincing everyone around us that we were okay. In fact, hey, we were doing great! Kasi turned inward, and I hid in busyness. We kept it spiritual and repeated lies to ourselves that sounded very Christian. We told everyone, "God won't give us more than we can handle. We just need to work harder and try to have more faith." But we were playing a most dangerous game.

Kasi was sad, angry, and even bitter. I was aloof and was romanticizing the "superspiritual" thing we'd done. However, inwardly we both knew this was not what we'd wanted. We'd wanted to come home with a perfectly healthy child. Kasi and I had filled out a checklist of special needs we were open to when adopting. This checklist ranged from learning disabilities to HIV to the inability to walk or talk, and I am sad to say we were not open to much on the list. *God, You didn't honor our checklist, and that really ticks us off!* Yes, we both had overflowing thought bubbles above our heads.

During this extremely challenging year, a steady flow of well-meaning Christian clichés flew our way, but they had little to no impact on our daily lives. No, I take that back. The clichés had a very high impact—in fact, they stirred a lot of annoyance and guilt, which is a nice way of saying they drove us completely nuts. While we tried to hold on to truth like "God is in control. He is with us. He has not forgotten us. He is doing all things for His glory and our good," those statements were being drowned out by pop psychology one-liners that aren't Christian at all but have been adopted by Christians, integrated into their belief systems, and are now a part of the Christian vernacular. Kasi and I were wrestling to separate what we knew to be truth from what we'd allowed to creep into our thoughts. We had both been to Bible college. I have four degrees in biblical studies, church history, theology, and Christian counseling. I'd read dozens upon dozens of books on Christian doctrine and orthodox beliefs. As a preacher of the Word of God, I would preach verse by verse through the Scriptures. However, when all hell broke loose in our lives, we chose to be entrapped by common lies instead of finding freedom in biblical truth. As a family, we were not prepared to walk in freedom in the midst of suffering. At this point, we were mad! Maybe we were mad because we were confronted with our own entrapment, or maybe we were mad that God was in control and not us. The bottom line is, we were mad.

At the same time, we felt guilty that we were struggling, hurting, and wanting to be in control. *Please, Lord, if You're really in control, could You control people to stop telling us lies that make it seem as though we are in control and You're just here to make us happy?*

The game went on until Kasi and I broke. We shattered, and for a season we simply fell apart. The common superficial lies that we believe as Christians and pass off to one another as truth were not the least bit helpful when things got really hard. They were like sand to a thirsty man.

Truth, Freedom, and Intact Flowerpots

Back to the backyard. As I was throwing my aforementioned hissy fit, Kasi sat down to talk to a friend who also has a special-needs child. She gave Kasi advice that would change everything for us. She said, "It's okay to grieve. You have to. What you imagined you were getting is not what you got, and it's okay to be sad. Be honest before the Lord. He knows how you feel anyway. You may be able to convince everyone else you are okay, but He knows you are not. Stop with the canned clichés you think you're supposed to say and others want to hear and get authentic and real about what is going on inside you."

We had convinced ourselves that we had to be okay. After all, we were not only Christians but also Christian leaders. We're supposed to put on a happy face no matter what and toss around a bunch of one-liners that sound spiritual, right?

No, that's not right. Not at all. Kasi and I decided to stop playing the game. We committed to move past the religious jargon and turn our focus back to the intended truth of the Word of God. Once we dug deeper than what cultural Christianity has to offer, we began to get real with the Scriptures again. Thankfully, this caused us to be honest about our struggles and become authentically unafraid to speak about our failures and letdowns. Then and only then did we begin to walk in freedom, the sweet freedom that brings the beautiful comfort and transformational power to walk through any storm and face any mountain. The truth of God's Word reminded us that God is doing all things for His glory and our good. It's only in this freedom that we can truly experience a peace that is beyond understanding. Now, please hear me: It wasn't like the clouds parted, angels started singing, and everyone lived happily ever after. Our season of life was still hard. But instead of playing a game, we began to live honestly before God, each other, and the people around us. And that's made all the difference.

My hope is that the pages of this book are an invitation for you to do the same. Together, let's tackle head-on the most common lies Christians believe today. You know, the ones that cause our faith to lose its voice of relevance, power, and effectiveness. Some of the lies we'll address are based on incorrect views of Scripture, and they hinder our spiritual maturity because we are not walking in truth. Other lies deeply affect our thinking and actions because we have forgotten what the Bible teaches about the character of God. Then there are lies Christians believe that are not based on Scripture at all. Rather, they are cultural teachings and spiritual-sounding clichés that snuck into the church, got baptized, and then joined the ranks of actual truth. But regardless of the kind, these lies are all enslaving.

Why the Jackalope?

Tales of rabbits with horns can be traced back to the thirteenth century. However, this mythical animal was popularized in

Wyoming in the 1930s when two brothers with taxidermy skills grafted deer antlers onto jackrabbit carcasses. They sold the combination to local hotels and retailers. Over recent decades, the jackalope has grown into a symbol of folklore, urban legends, and fables—much like Sasquatch, the Loch Ness monster, and the chupacabra.

Unique characteristics have been attributed to this horned varmint, such as being so dangerous that hunters are encouraged to wear shin guards on their legs to keep from being gored by this cantankerous creature. Another legend teaches that this elusive minibeast causes tons of confusion and chaos because it can imitate the human voice. This legend was popular during the days of the Old West when cowboys would gather around the campfire and sing at night—the jackalopes would allegedly join the choir by singing along as tenors.* Interestingly, some researchers believe the creation of the jackalope can be tied to sightings of rabbits that were infected with a very real and life-threatening virus that caused large tumors to grow on the head, resembling horns and antlers.

Jackalopes are like many of the lies Christians believe. The clichés we hear may seem harmless, innocent, or even cute in the moment. However, we need to realize what they are—lies. And if they are believed for too long, they may become a very dangerous virus to our faith.

What's the best way to deconstruct a lie? Shine the light of truth on it. So we're going to return to the basics of who God is by

---

* "Jackalope," Wikipedia, last modified June 15, 2018, 22:20, https://en.wikipedia.org /wiki/Jackalope.

diving deeply into His Scriptures. "Now the Lord is the Spirit, and where the Spirit of the Lord is, there is freedom" (2 Corinthians 3:17). Freedom can be found where the Spirit is, and what does the Spirit stay close to? Truth. "You will know the truth, and the truth will set you free" (John 8:32). The road to the freedom God desires for us is found by walking in spirit and truth (see John 4:24). You can't have one without the other. Really.

God Won't Give Me More Than I Can Handle

Well, Actually . . .

"God won't give you more than you can handle." Yeah, right, tell that to Jay and Suzanne Faske. In the middle of 1990, they were sitting together watching a documentary on the orphanages in China. They were engaged to be married in January 1991. At that time, little did they know that what God was placing on their hearts would eventually lead to the adoption of many children—and when I say many, I mean over twenty.

By the time the Faskes had celebrated their five-year wedding anniversary, they had been through two miscarriages but had also been blessed with two biological sons. God gave them two beautiful babies to love, but the images of unwanted orphaned children still flooded their minds. At that very moment, they decided that if they were going to have more children, it would be through adoption. They remember saying that they were planning on having a big family one day, one with four children. That was probably the moment when God had a good belly laugh over their determined plans.

Often when we believe or regurgitate the statement "God won't give you more than you can handle," really what we're saying is that we don't want more than what we believe we can handle. If we're honest, we make plans for ourselves that keep us comfortable, and we want God to bless those plans and stay inside those boundaries. However, God hardly ever operates that way. He almost always gives us more than we can handle on our own so that we'll seek Him for help and guidance.

When the Faske boys were three and two years old, they were in a terrible accident. One of them sustained minor injuries, while the other had to be hospitalized for a dislocated hip and major lacerations to his legs. After going home, he spent six weeks in traction. Watching their son in so much pain opened their eyes to realize there are so many children in this world who go without the love of parents to comfort them or the medical care they desperately need when they are hurting. That accident proved to be a turning point for the family. It was time to start the adoption process. They soon left the States for India.

Like so many families who start the adoption process, Jay and Suzanne had a mental picture in their minds of how magical the moment would be when they met their child for the first time. Surely it would look something like them running across a field of flowers, jumping into one another's arms, and hugging necks while twirling in the wind. That would be something they could handle. But instead, their story turned out to be forty-nine children running their way, screaming and pulling on their legs, while one frightened little girl ran crying in the opposite direction. That little girl eventually became their daughter! The experience of living a life they could not handle started to become more real to them when they got on a plane to bring their baby girl home and a man asked to be moved away from her, stating that she was cursed because she had a cleft lip and palate.

A few months later, they were on their way back to India to adopt another child, this time a little boy. They believed their family was now complete. It was perfect. This is what they had planned. They believed they could handle this. God had answered their prayers. Amen.

But these were *their* plans, not the Lord's. God is good at giving us more than we can handle. Before long, the Faske family was at it again after hearing about a sibling group of three in Russia who desperately needed a home and a family—two boys and a girl. Surely now their family was complete, right? Nope. Their family would keep getting bigger.

As the Faske family continued to grow, so did their influence in the lives of others. They approached their church family about starting an orphan ministry to help find families for orphans around the world. At this same time, they were asked to consider coordinating a summer host program for older orphaned children. That summer they watched God work in a very powerful way as they helped almost forty children join their forever families. They had stepped into an area that was unfamiliar to them. You could even say it was overwhelming and more than they could handle. Until this point, the oldest child they had adopted was six years old. However, most of the children they had begun working with were between the ages of eleven and fifteen. These children had been through some of the most horrific things you could imagine and had come from the darkest places on the planet. Not only was the Faske family exposed to more than they could handle, but these children had experienced a life that was more than anyone should have to handle. Very quickly, the line that "God won't give you more than you can handle" was being uncovered as a lie, plain and simple.

As these hurting children who had experienced so much trauma were being incorporated into families, it became clear that some of them might never attach and bond fully to their new surroundings. Even though all the host and adoptive families were required to go through training, there was nothing that could prepare them for some of the challenges they would face. As the wheels began to fall off and families couldn't cope any longer, the Faske home became a refuge for children whose adoptive families could no longer continue to parent them.

All these scenarios, woven together by an intentional God, created a very unique story for the Faske family. The description "big family" would be an understatement for them. Jay and Suzanne have twenty-eight children: twenty-five through adoption and three who are biologically theirs. This family is nearly equivalent to the diversity of the United Nations. Their children are from India, Russia, China, Kazakhstan, Colombia, Ethiopia, and the United States. When the Summer or Winter Olympics are being held, this family wins because they have so many countries representing them!

"Well, you know what the Bible says: 'God won't give you

more than you can handle.'" I can imagine the Faske family hearing that and bursting into laughter. Twenty-eight children? Plus the adoption process itself? Then dealing with the trauma the kids experienced and overcoming cultural differences and barriers from seven different countries? Yeah, right.

I know, I know. Using the Faske family as an example is a pretty extreme way to expose this lie. But let's look at "God won't give you more than you can handle" in a little more detail. First of all, this statement cannot be found anywhere in the Bible. Most people who say it claim it's because they've heard others use it. But as far as it being something God actually said? No, it's not in there.

Now, some people might point to 1 Corinthians 10 as justification for the statement: "Let anyone who thinks that he stands take heed lest he fall. No temptation has overtaken you that is not common to man. God is faithful, and he will not let you be tempted beyond your ability, but with the temptation he will also provide the way of escape, that you may be able to endure it" (verses 12–13). Sounds a little similar, right? However, context is key here, and these verses are talking specifically about temptation. Basically, the verses are teaching that everyone is tempted. Each one of us has different weaknesses and different enticements that will grab our attention, but the point is that we will all face temptation. So when temptation comes, we need to have a game plan in place. The promise we have from God in those moments is that we will not be tempted beyond our ability to overcome it. Yet we still need God in those very moments. Notice the comforts given: "God is faithful" and "he will also provide the way of escape." Even in this scenario it's more than we can handle, because we are completely dependent on God to keep His promises. For example, when that inappropriate image pops up on your computer screen, the way of escape is the power button. When gossip springs up at your office, the way of escape is shutting it down or walking away. God remains faithful to provide the way of escape and therefore gives us the ability to endure temptation when it comes our way.

If you think about it, all of life is more than we can handle. We don't exist without a God who creates us. We don't breathe without the breath He places in our lungs. We can't comprehend and make decisions without the brain He has given us. We can't feel, love, and care without the heart and soul He has placed inside us. We can't navigate through this journey called life without the wisdom that comes from Him. We can't endure suffering without a God who gives us hope of a brighter tomorrow and a promise that He has a plan and purpose for everything and everyone. We can't truly heal unless there is a God who can heal us.

Yes, all of life is more than we can handle. But it is not more than God can handle through us.

God Won't Give You More Than He Can Handle Through You

One of the greatest promises that God gives us in Scripture is not that He will keep us out of difficult situations or that He will make sure we never experience suffering. Rather, He promises to be with us in those difficult situations and be an ever-present help in times of suffering. "God is our refuge and strength, a very present help in trouble" (Psalm 46:1).

He also doesn't promise us that we'll face only things we can handle. If we were able to handle everything in life on our own, then why would we need God? Often the biggest blessing of being in over our heads in life is that we have an opportunity to rely on a God who can take on anything and everything. He is able. "Fear not, for I am with you; be not dismayed, for I am your God; I will strengthen you, I will help you, I will uphold you with my righteous right hand" (Isaiah 41:10).

The promise is not that He won't give you more than you can handle but rather that He won't give you more than He can handle through you. As overwhelming as the Faske family's life appears to be, they have learned the valuable lesson of depending on their Lord for the power to live a life that glorifies Him and helps others. This hasn't always been easy or natural for them. There have been times when trusting in the Lord was a real struggle. As their family grew over the years, not everyone was as supportive as you'd hope they would be of a family who has helped so many. It's a hard thing to handle when you feel as if you're obeying God and being a blessing to others and yet you endure a barrage of negative comments. They'd hear things such as, "How can you possibly love that many children? How do you have the time? Why would you choose this? How can you afford to raise that many children?"

However, if everything that comes with being a family of thirty, plus receiving some pretty disheartening comments, seems like a lot to handle, there would be even more. A day. The day. April 23, 2017, would bring a change that once again proved this life always has turns and difficulties that are too much to handle.

That day a few of the Faske children rose from bed early in the morning and headed to a cattle show in Rockdale, Texas. After the show, Nathaniel, now living on his own, dropped his siblings off at home, then headed toward his new place of residence. Sadly, he never made it.

Mr. Faske and one of the sons were fishing in the pond in front of their house, and Mrs. Faske walked down to the pond to sit on the dock with them. Shortly after, a police officer showed up at their gate. At first they thought he was trying to turn around, but then he moved closer, as if he wanted to come in. Mr. Faske went to meet him, and his wife could see them talking. The officer passed Mr. Faske the wallet that belonged to Nathaniel, and in that moment Mrs. Faske knew. She dropped to her knees and begged God not to let this happen, to bring their son back. There was no way they could handle this. No person should have to. Kids are supposed to bury their parents, not the other way around.

Nathaniel had fallen asleep at the wheel and lost control of his car. He was only twenty-one years old—too young to leave this earth. He had been a part of the Faske family since they adopted him from Russia when he was six. When he joined the family, he had a hardened look in his eyes. He had been through a lot and was filled with pain. He didn't know how to express everything he had been through and wasn't sure he liked the idea of letting the Faskes be his parents. Over time, he softened and grew into a wonderful young man, the kind of guy who would be there for others when they needed him, no matter what he was doing. He was the type of person who paid attention to what others liked and then showed up with the perfect surprise. But on April 23, all that ended. Nathaniel died way too soon, and now this family of twenty-nine was feeling the heavy weight of sorrow, loss, and heartache. It was more than they could ever handle on their own.

The next few days were a blur for the Faske family. Just as for any loss of a loved one, there were many arrangements to be made for the funeral. As difficult as it was for the parents to process, they also had a lot of little ones who didn't understand what had happened to their older brother. How do parents who have lost a child in a horrible accident help their other children understand why this happened when they can't even understand it themselves?

Surely everything was about to calm down for the Faske family. It would have to, right? What else could this family possibly face? They slowly tried to return to a routine. About a month later, they attempted to have a typical family day on their farm, riding horses and going swimming in the lake near their house. The kids were really excited because this was the first thing they had done that seemed normal since their brother's death. They saddled eighteen horses and prepared for a short trail ride to the lake. Two of the daughters, Lily and Cherish, were the last two kids to get on their horses. Cherish was only six years old and needed help getting on, so Lily was helping her. It's crazy how things can change in a heartbeat. As Lily put Cherish on the horse, the horse moved in a way that jerked one of the reins from Cherish's hands. As the rein hit the ground, the horse stepped on it, panicked, and began backing up in such a hurry that the horse tripped over backward. The horse fell on top of Cherish with such force that it knocked itself out and injured Cherish badly. When the horse came to, it started paddling in a circle on its side while Lily pulled

Cherish out from under it. Suddenly, a peaceful routine day turned into ambulances, emergency lights, and medical workers filling the driveway.

While Mr. Faske and one of the grown sons tried to restrain the horse, Mrs. Faske held her little girl's face and screamed for her to keep breathing. Praise God, she had been wearing a helmet, but her chest had been crushed by the saddle horn. Cherish kept falling asleep, and it was obvious she was dying. When her mother could get her to wake up, Cherish would say, "Mommy, I don't want to die."

"God won't give you more than you can handle." Yeah, right. As a loving parent in this scenario, you would have to think and plead with the Lord, *Not again. How can this be happening again? This is too much!* With these thoughts rolling around in Mrs. Faske's head, she told her daughter, "Just pray, sweetie. Pray to Jesus. Keep praying to Jesus, Cherish."

What seemed like hours for this fragile family was probably less than thirty-five minutes. The ambulance took them to a location where they met a helicopter that transported them to a hospital. As they were loading Cherish onto the helicopter, they heard one of the medical workers say, "I know this family. They lost their son just one month ago. Please do everything you can for her." Cherish immediately went into surgery at the hospital when the helicopter landed. She spent about two weeks in the intensive care unit, but now she is a healthy and happy little girl.

Without a doubt, the Faskes are some of the most incredible people my wife and I have ever met. The first time we heard their story in its entirety, we were blown away, to say the least. I'll never forget them talking about the pithy statements people shared with them. Statements we've all heard—and most of the time hated.

During their most difficult days, people would tell them, "You know, God will never give you more than you can handle." The truth is that God is sovereign. If we trust that He is sovereign in the good, then we also need to trust that He is sovereign when we think things are bad. He is in control, and His timing is perfect. It's not always easy. Sometimes it is more than we can cope with on our own, but it is still perfect.

> For everything there is a season, and a time for every
>> matter under heaven:
>> a time to be born, and a time to die;
>> a time to plant, and a time to pluck up what is planted;
>> a time to kill, and a time to heal;
>> a time to break down, and a time to build up;
>> a time to weep, and a time to laugh;
>> a time to mourn, and a time to dance.
>> (Ecclesiastes 3:1–4)

The Faske family can tell you from firsthand experience that they believe God has given them far more than they can handle, but they're still leaning on Him. They trust He will never give them more than He can handle through them. Even in the most extreme circumstances, He has carried them through it all. They have survived because of His grace. They can't explain it, but sometimes the greatest gifts are those you can't explain. There's just a peace, even in the midst of the storm. It's a storm you can't handle, and yet you still endure. Why? Because He is with you. Somehow you feel the strength to stand firm because you're standing on Him as your foundation. "He said to me, 'My grace is sufficient for you, for my power is made perfect in weakness.' Therefore I will boast all the more gladly of my weaknesses, so that the power of Christ may rest upon me. For the sake of Christ, then, I am content with weaknesses, insults, hardships, persecutions, and calamities. For when I am weak, then I am strong" (2 Corinthians 12:9–10).

God chooses what to reveal to us and what not to reveal. The primary truths He has revealed to us are that He loves us, is with us, and can identify with us. No matter what we're going through, He can handle it. We can't, but He can. One of the main reasons He can handle whatever we're going through is because He is a God who can identify with His creation.

A Great God Who Identifies with You

We've all said it, or at least thought it: "Jesus couldn't possibly understand what I'm going through right now. After all, He never had to experience what I am dealing with!" Often, this thought is brought on by physical suffering, feelings of being alone, or thinking you are the only one who has had to wrestle with a particular temptation, trial, or conflict. In a way, this thought process has been made worse by a common reading of Scripture that skips right from the birth of Jesus to His death and resurrection, ignoring the fact that most of the Gospels deal with Jesus's life—His very human life. The truth is, if there's anybody who can understand what you're going through, it's Jesus.

When the Son of God came to earth two thousand years ago, He was fully God, but He was also fully human. In Jesus, the qualities of God and the qualities of mankind were slammed together into One. With this reality came all the experiences of what it means to be human—the good, the bad, and the ugly. Therefore, He can completely identify with everything humans go through. He personally knows what it's like to suffer and experience hardships. He understands and can empathize with you in ways no one else can.

Let's take a look at some of the very familiar yet very incredible ways that Jesus identifies with us in our humanity.

Jesus Knew What It Was Like to Experience Poverty

Living from paycheck to paycheck can be a very real struggle for anyone. Surely God can't understand what it is like to go to sleep hungry and cold, can He? Well, Jesus, the Son of God, knew exactly what it was like to be poor. After all, He was homeless, so He can identify with those who have to do without. "Foxes have holes, and birds of the air have nests, but the Son of Man has nowhere to lay his head" (Luke 9:58).

Jesus Knew What It Was Like to Experience Exhaustion

It's okay to admit it: some days, maybe even most days, we're T-I-R-E-D tired. Jesus knew all too well what it was like to experience weariness. It's good to remind ourselves that Jesus walked everywhere He went. On top of that, He had to deal with His disciples arguing about who was the greatest while often completely missing whatever lesson He was trying to teach them in that moment. Not to mention having religious leaders plotting His death while He did nothing but good, such as healing people, raising folks from the dead, and feeding the hungry. Many times He would keep on walking and go off by Himself to pray. He knows what it is like to be physically and emotionally exhausted, and He knows what the remedy is.

Jesus Knew What It Was Like to Be Betrayed

Unfortunately, Jesus was well acquainted with the pain of betrayal. Not only was He betrayed by religious leaders who were jealous of the crowds that were following Him, but He was also betrayed by those very close to Him. For example, His own family! "When his family heard it, they went out to seize him, for they were saying, 'He is out of his mind'" (Mark 3:21). One of His closest friends also betrayed Him: "Immediately the rooster crowed a second time. And Peter remembered how Jesus had said to him, 'Before the rooster crows twice, you will deny me three times.' And he broke down and wept" (Mark 14:72). And ultimately one of the Twelve sold Him out for thirty pieces of silver. "[He] said, 'What will you give me if I deliver him over to you?' And they paid him thirty pieces of silver" (Matthew 26:15).

Jesus Knew What It Was Like to Suffer from Grief

Jesus knew what it was like to experience heartache, sadness, and sorrow. A couple of instances in the Gospels show Jesus weeping, first over the condition of Jerusalem: "And when he drew near and saw the city, he wept over it" (Luke 19:41), and second due to His grief at the death of a beloved friend: "Jesus wept" (John 11:35). He was also sorrowed by humanity's rejection of God: "He was despised and rejected by men, a man of sorrows and acquainted with grief; and as one from whom men hide their faces he was despised, and we esteemed him not" (Isaiah 53:3).

Jesus Knew What It Was Like to Be Tempted

Maybe you can accept that Jesus knew grief and exhaustion, but when it comes to fighting temptation, surely Jesus cannot relate. But the writer of Hebrews reminds us that nothing could be further from the truth. Although Jesus never committed a sin, He was still tempted. Therefore, "because he himself has suffered when tempted, he is able to help those who are being tempted" (2:18).

Jesus Knew What It Was Like to Experience Suffering

When we search for meaning in our suffering, it can be hard to find on this side of eternity because we cannot know all the purposes of a sovereign God. But we have a savior who knew exactly what it was like to suffer. He confided His emotional pain to His disciples, saying, "My soul is very sorrowful, even to death" (Matthew 26:38). And He obviously endured the physical pain of His extremely gruesome death on the cross.

Jesus Knew What It Was Like to Feel Forsaken by God

Even when we feel as though God has forsaken us, Jesus can identify. God the Father had to turn His face away from His Son while

He became sin on the cross in our place. "About the ninth hour Jesus cried out with a loud voice, saying, 'Eli, Eli, lema sabach-thani?' that is, 'My God, my God, why have you forsaken me?'" (Matthew 27:46). However, we need to remember that although it was a reality for Jesus at that time, being forsaken by God is only a feeling for His children. The truth is, He has told us, "I will never leave you nor forsake you" (Hebrews 13:5).

Plain and simple, Jesus knows what it's like to live as a human. He got hungry. He got thirsty. He slept. He had to learn things. He grew. He loved. He was glad. He was angry. He was troubled at times. He prayed. He exercised faith. He read the Scriptures. He hurt when He saw another person's illness. He cried when He saw death. As the old hymn "What a Friend We Have in Jesus" says, "Jesus knows our every weakness."

What a massive comfort to know that "we do not have a high priest who is unable to sympathize with our weaknesses, but one who in every respect has been tempted as we are, yet without sin" (Hebrews 4:15). Yes, Jesus knows.

He Is Your Strength

You will experience the ebb and flow of life. Ups and downs. Good days and bad days. Times when everything makes sense and times when nothing makes sense. There will be seasons when you have resources at your disposal to pay all your bills early, and then there will be other times when you look at your bank account and start pleading for Jesus to come back before that bill is due. Life throws a ton at you. It's a lot to bear. It's more than you can handle on your own. But it is not more than He can handle, because He has already experienced it Himself and conquered it. Trust in Him. Find your strength in Him. Relying on Jesus means you don't have to figure out how to be victorious over rough times, because His victory will be your victory. Rest in that truth. Walk in that freedom.

Hopefully you'll get to live a full life and live long enough to get the senior discount at restaurants. When you approach the last chapter of your life here on earth, the goal is to be able to say something similar to what the apostle Paul penned to the believers at Philippi: "Not that I am speaking of being in need, for I have learned in whatever situation I am to be content. I know how to be brought low, and I know how to abound. In any and every circumstance, I have learned the secret of facing plenty and hunger, abundance and need. I can do all things through him who strengthens me" (Philippians 4:11–13). No matter what Paul was going through, he had learned how to remain content. Why was he able to be content regardless of the circumstances around him? The answer was that he had a secret (see verse 12). What was his secret? Well, verse 13 is the secret.

Philippians 4:13 has to be one of the most misquoted and misused verses in all of the Bible: "I can do all things through him who strengthens me." This verse has nothing to do with dunking a basketball, hitting a game-winning home run, bench-pressing a bus, winning the lottery, or closing a business deal. On the other hand, in its context, this is an extremely helpful and encouraging verse. When the apostle Paul wrote these words, he was under house arrest awaiting his trial, where he might possibly be put to death for preaching the resurrection of Jesus. However, instead of being defeated by unfortunate circumstances, Paul used this opportunity to teach the young church in Philippi that he could endure any and every circumstance—ups and downs, highs and lows—because he had a strength that comes only from Christ. This supernatural strength to endure all seasons and situations was always with Paul because the Holy Spirit of Christ was always with him, even in prison.

Just ask the Faske family. They have learned by experience, through the good and the bad times, that Christ is always there with them. They have suffered more than any family should. They have taken on more than anyone else I can think of. And yet, through these times of highs and lows, God has molded them. Each of their adoptions has come with its own challenges, but the blessings have outweighed the struggles. The life transformations they have seen in their children, and in the lives of others around them, are unmeasurable. Suffering has brought their family closer together and has given each member of their family compassion for others who have experienced extreme hurt. God has given the Faske family much more than they could handle. It hasn't all been pretty, but it has definitely been beautiful.

Questions for Common Lie 1

1. Before reading this chapter, what came to your mind when you heard the statement "God won't give you more than you can handle"?

2. Read 1 Corinthians 10:12–13. What promises are made in those verses? What does God want you to know about Him from those verses? What are some examples of ways of escape in the midst of temptation?

3. The story of the Faske family is an extreme example of going through difficult situations and seasons of life. You may not experience what they did, but you will experience your own struggles. Recall your most recent significant struggle (you may still be in it). Was your faith strong or weak during that time?

4. How did this chapter change or reinforce your view of God? How did it change or reinforce how you view struggles and suffering? How did it change or reinforce how you view faith?

5. How did the examples of how Jesus can identify with your life experiences change or reinforce your view of Jesus?

A Truth to Move Forward With

Sometimes God gives us more than we can handle, but He never gives us more than He can handle through us.

God Gained Another Angel

And the Terrible, Horrible, No Good, Very Bad Day

I have a dear friend named Dean. He is one of the greatest men you've probably never heard of, but you'd be better for it if you had. Dean is, in my opinion, a modern-day Job. You remember Job, right? From the Bible? Job was a wealthy man living in the land of Uz with a large family, lots of land, and enough livestock to make the San Diego Zoo keepers envious. He was well respected in his community and considered "blameless" and "upright," always careful to avoid doing evil (Job 1:1). Then one day Satan decided to challenge God's worth by attacking one of His choicest servants. You guessed who—Job. This was only after God had boasted to Satan about Job's character. You see, Satan believed the only reason Job worshipped God and walked in integrity was because he was richly blessed. God replied, essentially, "All right. Try him."

And along came Job's terrible, horrible, no good, very bad day. You're familiar with *Alexander and the Terrible, Horrible,*

No Good, Very Bad Day, right? The children's story? It's the story of a little boy named Alexander whose day brings with it a string of disappointments, like finding chewing gum in his hair, having no prize in his breakfast cereal, the dentist discovering a cavity, his mom serving lima beans for dinner, and the list goes on. For a little boy, sure, that all stinks. But Job was not a little boy, and his story is far from fictional.

In the course of a single day, Job received message after message, each one bringing more bad news. Throughout Job's terrible, horrible, no good, very bad day, he lost all his livestock, most of his servants, and all ten of his children. I'm not kidding.

Can you imagine? You lose all your earthly possessions, and naturally your mind would go into fix-it mode. You'd immediately start thinking about how you're going to rebound, and you would begin frantically searching for the phone number for your insurance agency. It's hard, but you can cope. You can rebuild. Then here comes the crushing news that no amount of insurance or rebuilding efforts could fix. Your precious children—the ones who are supposed to bury you—are gone, all gone.

No parent should have to endure this. What is Job going to do? Surely, if anyone has a right to shake his fists at heaven and curse God, it's Job. Everyone is watching. What is he going to do? His wife is watching. His friends and neighbors are all watching. The angels are watching. Satan is watching. All eyes are on the man God believes in.

Job tears his clothes and shaves his head as a sign of extreme heartbreak and emotional suffering. Then he falls. He falls to the ground and worships! What? How could it be? How is that even possible? Yes, Job worships. "And he said, 'Naked I came from my mother's womb, and naked shall I return. The LORD gave, and the LORD has taken away; blessed be the name of the LORD.' In all this Job did not sin or charge God with wrong" (1:21–22). God is still worthy of praise and worship, even on the most terrible, horrible, no good, very bad day. As hard as it was, Job took a journey over the next weeks, months, and years, learning more and more that God is always in control. Job had always heard about God and believed in Him. But now Job's relationship moved to a deeper level of actually seeing God and His purposes. "I had heard of you by the hearing of the ear, but now my eye sees you" (42:5).

God Is Gaining Angels?

Well, my dear friend Dean reminds me of Job. No, he never lost hordes of sheep, camels, and donkeys. But he has known terrible, horrible, no good, very bad days all too well. Dean's first wife, Lynne, was diagnosed with pancreatic cancer. He cared for her, prayed for her, and watched her suffer for eleven long months. They prayed together, believed together, and trusted in the Scriptures together. Over the months, as cancer ate away at her body, their faith never wavered. Dean and Lynne printed off Bible verses to place throughout their house—on mirrors, doors, and kitchen cabinets. Daily, they would read these verses and hold on to them as precious jewels. Verses such as,

> Blessed be the God and Father of our Lord Jesus Christ,
> the Father of mercies and God of all comfort, who

comforts us in all our affliction, so that we may be able
to comfort those who are in any affliction, with the
comfort with which we ourselves are comforted by God.
(2 Corinthians 1:3–4)

Fear not, for I am with you;
   be not dismayed, for I am your God;
I will strengthen you, I will help you,
   I will uphold you with my righteous right hand. (Isaiah
     41:10)

Do not be anxious about anything, but in everything by
prayer and supplication with thanksgiving let your
requests be made known to God. And the peace of God,
which surpasses all understanding, will guard your hearts
and your minds in Christ Jesus. (Philippians 4:6–7)

Then the day came that would be devastating for any loving
husband. July 27 was the day that God took Lynne home. Just
four days shy of their twelfth wedding anniversary. But Dean was
not the only one in the home left behind. There were also two
young boys: nine-year-old Elliot—smart, kind, and athletic—
and eight-year-old Evan—sweet, determined, and living with special needs.

As a single dad, Dean raised both of his boys to love Jesus, to
faithfully attend church, and to always love and serve others, even
in the midst of loss, heartache, and sorrow. He worshipped God
anyway. He believed that God was still worthy of praise. This

husband never believed that his wife lost her battle with cancer. Cancer did not win. No, it was God who called her home, and cancer was just the avenue of getting her there. Lynne finished her race. She won, because her victory was in Christ. She is now with Him, free, healed, and perfectly whole. Dean believes this, and he taught his boys to believe and understand this truth as well.

One day, after being single for over two and a half years, his eyes caught another beauty. Her name was Kristal. After Dean and Kristal spent some time together, God began to enkindle a love in him for another woman—this godly woman. Kristal had two kids of her own—a boy and a girl. This blended family became a happy, unified home. Of course, they experienced the normal pains, difficulties, and struggles that any parents do when their children go through their teenage years. But this was a godly family who were highly involved in a local church. And the faith didn't belong just to the parents. All the kids had a faith of their own and were active participants in the church's student ministry. Each one had a loving and vibrant relationship with Jesus. All was well, very well.

I don't believe you truly ever get over the death of a loved one. A heart that is broken can heal, but the scars and wounds of an extreme loss will always be there. Nevertheless, you can have hope, confidence, and strength to begin living a new normal.

Just as Dean was hitting his stride in his new normal, the calendar page turned to May 31, 2011. His oldest son, Elliot, was attending his girlfriend's high school graduation. Elliot had graduated a year earlier with grades and accomplishments that any parent would be proud of. He was a standout baseball player on the varsity team, was a leader in his church's student ministry, and had even surrendered his life at a Christian youth camp, vowing to use the rest of his days serving Jesus and the church. His goals were to go to a Christian college to become a youth pastor and then eventually to become a lead pastor at a church.

After the graduation ceremony was over, friends and family were standing around Elliot and his girlfriend. Lots of plans for the future were being made. Then came the moment that changed all those plans. Elliot passed out. Fainted. In front of everyone gathered around. Before anyone could react, his head hit the floor.

Elliot was taken to the hospital, where doctors found a pilocytic astrocytoma, a type of brain tumor. As shocking and sobering as this discovery was to his friends and family, there was still hope that everything would be okay. Elliot went through thirty days of radiation and two surgeries. It took some time, but he returned to his normal life of hopes and dreams and goals.

Then it happened again. Four years later, there was another fainting spell. Another visit to the hospital. Another brain tumor. This time the pilocytic astrocytoma had turned into glioblastoma, with a brain tumor that proved to be inoperable. Every day friends and family prayed for healing. Without a doubt, God can do that. He heals people every day, but then there are other times, for reasons we don't understand, when He chooses not to. One of the greatest mysteries in this world is why God chooses to heal some here on earth and not to heal others. It's in those moments when we're asked to trust, even when we can't see.

Elliot fought his cancer for months. God taught me so much

through this young man and his father, Dean. Their confidence in the plans of God and their hope of life beyond earth was absolutely amazing to witness. In the times when I was crushed by Elliot's suffering, they were the rocks. The two people who were hit the hardest—Elliot and Dean—were the ones who hit back the hardest with their faith. Obviously, Dean had experienced this before with his first wife, and even though his heart was broken watching his son suffer, he was still a rock. I believe the Holy Spirit gives people going through extreme suffering a special grace that extends them a hope, peace, and confidence that goes well beyond their natural abilities. "He gives power to the faint, and to him who has no might he increases strength" (Isaiah 40:29).

As Elliot's body continually grew weaker, his confidence in God only grew stronger. His faith never wavered. Personally, I'll never forget visiting Elliot and his family in his last days. My intent was to go there to encourage them, but inevitably I always left with tears in my eyes, encouraged by this amazing family.

Then the terrible, horrible, no good, very bad day came. Elliot died.

What do you tell a family who is seemingly doing everything right yet is hit with such heartache and loss? What do you tell a man like Dean Davis, who saw cancer take both his first wife and then his son? Seriously, what do you say?

On more than one occasion, with a well-intentioned heart and a stuttering mouth, I've heard Christians respond with some variation of "Well, God gained another angel today." But did He really? Is that true?

According to the CIA World Factbook, on average, there are approximately 151,600 deaths every single day.* So does that mean God is receiving over 150,000 new angels every day? I'm not trying to be funny here or hard on Christians who are trying to comfort the grieving. But it's important to know the truth about the afterlife because sharing a lie with people who are heartbroken is of no help to them. No matter how well intentioned the lie is, it is still a lie. What people need the most on their terrible, horrible, no good, very bad days is the comforting truth of God's Word.

God Is Not Gaining Angels;
He Is Calling Home Believers

So what is the comforting truth of God's Word? I'm glad you asked. Here it is, plain and simple: humans are humans, and angels are angels. This remains so even in eternity. In fact, angels are intrigued by the interaction between God and His image-bearing humans: "It was revealed to them that they were serving not themselves but you, in the things that have now been announced to you through those who preached the good news to you by the Holy Spirit sent from heaven, things into which angels long to look" (1 Peter 1:12).

It's actually better for you to be human than to be an angel. Most Bible scholars believe that the scriptural accounts of Ezekiel 28:12–18, Isaiah 14:12–14, and Revelation 12:4 describe the fall of Lucifer (a former angel) and one-third of the angels (now con-

---

* The World Factbook, cited by Ecology Global Network, www.ecology.com /birth-death-rates/.

sidered demons) that joined his revolt against God. What's sobering about the accounts of these fallen angels is that their judgments were final, with no hope of redemption, forgiveness, or grace. I believe this is what Peter was discussing when he wrote "things into which angels long to look." Angels are astonished by God's unconditional love for you!

You can see in the Bible that angels play some very important roles. They are God's messengers. In fact, the word *angel* means "messenger of God." Time and time again, there are instances in Scripture when an angel delivered a message on behalf of God. Here are just a few of the many people in the Bible who were visited by angels with a message: Hagar (see Genesis 16), Balaam (see Numbers 22), Joshua (see Joshua 5), Zechariah (see Luke 1), and Peter (see Acts 10), not to mention Mary, the mother of Jesus (see Luke 1), and then Joseph, Jesus's earthly father (see Matthew 1).

Angels are also protectors of God's people. An angel shut the mouths of the lions in the presence of Daniel: "My God sent his angel and shut the lions' mouths, and they have not harmed me" (Daniel 6:22). An angel opened the prison doors to set the disciples of Jesus free after they were arrested for preaching His resurrection: "During the night an angel of the Lord opened the prison doors and brought them out" (Acts 5:19).

Like you and me, angels are created to worship God. The prophet Isaiah got to peek into the throne room of God through a vision and saw angels worshipping the Lord perfectly: "And one called to another and said: 'Holy, holy, holy is the LORD of hosts; the whole earth is full of his glory!'" (Isaiah 6:3).

Finally, angels are God's warriors. They are extremely powerful!

In fact, in 2 Kings there is an account of one angel wiping out over 185,000 Assyrian soldiers: "That night the angel of the LORD went out and struck down 185,000 in the camp of the Assyrians. And when people arose early in the morning, behold, these were all dead bodies" (19:35). Incredible, right? One against 185,000. Doesn't sound like the doll-faced porcelain angels we saw at Grandma's house, does it? These beings are fierce and strong. And the Lord has legions of them on His side! He truly is the God of angel armies.

However, as great as angels are, God did not send Jesus for them. God so loved humans that He sent His Son to become a human (although He never stopped being God) to die as a human for humans! What great love God has for us as human beings: "God shows his love for us in that while we were still sinners, Christ died for us" (Romans 5:8). Christ died for people, not angels. Through His resurrection, Jesus conquered sin and death for people, not angels. Through faith in the Son of God, we get to experience grace, hope, and complete forgiveness for our rebellion against Him. Angels never get to experience this!

Here is our ultimate hope: when a loved one dies knowing Jesus as his lord and savior, God does not gain another angel. Rather, God calls another worshipper to come home. Your loved one gets the opportunity to see Jesus face to face. He gets to leave this temporary place for his eternal home in the arms of his loving Father. You can have absolute peace knowing that God and His Word can be trusted. Let the promises of the Scriptures mend your broken heart, giving you confidence that your loved one, if he knew Jesus, is more alive today than you are—not as an angel but rather as a fully glorified human being with a perfect heart that is no longer susceptible to sin, a mind that is no longer susceptible to depression, and a body that is no longer susceptible to disease or death.

I love the way the apostle Paul described this to the believers in Thessalonica. These verses are an encouragement for us today as well.

> But we do not want you to be uninformed, brothers, about those who are asleep, that you may not grieve as others do who have no hope. For since we believe that Jesus died and rose again, even so, through Jesus, God will bring with him those who have fallen asleep. For this we declare to you by a word from the Lord, that we who are alive, who are left until the coming of the Lord, will not precede those who have fallen asleep. For the Lord himself will descend from heaven with a cry of command, with the voice of an archangel, and with the sound of the trumpet of God. And the dead in Christ will rise first. Then we who are alive, who are left, will be caught up together with them in the clouds to meet the Lord in the air, and so we will always be with the Lord. Therefore encourage one another with these words. (1 Thessalonians 4:13–18)

RIP . . . Maybe

You've seen it a thousand times. Well, I have seen it a thousand times. Especially when a celebrity athlete, musician, or actor passes away. Immediately, a barrage of epitaphs are posted on social media with the acronym RIP. Which, of course, means "rest in peace." I'm always amazed at how many Christians post this without really considering what they're saying or what their friends or coworkers will read in their sentiment. Now, we all know that no one can truly see what is in another person's heart. It is very possible that a particular celebrity did have a relationship with Jesus Christ as her lord and savior. However, I can think of times when an athlete passed away who was a very outspoken follower of a religion other than Christianity, or a musician died whose lifestyle was the opposite of how the Bible describes an authentic follower of Jesus. Yet even from Christians, the RIP statements were ever flowing.

But if we're going to commit to the truth, then we've got to be all in. The whole truth and nothing but the truth, even when it makes us uncomfortable. Especially in difficult moments of sadness and grief, people often check their faith at the door. However, it's in these moments when we need the truth of Scripture and the freedom it provides.

Truthfully, according to the Bible, the only ones who will get to rest in peace are those who have an authentic relationship with the Prince of Peace. Sadly, for those who have lived life without knowing Jesus as Lord and never had His Spirit dwell inside them, there will be no eternal rest. As gut wrenching as it is to write, their eternity will be marked by the very opposite of rest. Just as heaven is real, so also is hell.

Jesus Himself often used the word *Gehenna* to describe hell. The word literally meant "the Valley of the Son of Hinnom." I've personally seen this valley two different times in my travels through Israel. It is just south of Jerusalem. It is known as a cursed place. Some of the ancient Israelites sacrificed their children to false gods by burning them alive in this valley (see 2 Chronicles 28; 33; Jeremiah 19). In Jesus's day, it continued to be an unclean place used as the city dump. Gehenna was always on fire from the burning of trash. It was a place that people didn't even like to discuss because it was marked by sadness, maggots, fire, and curses. One day, Jesus used an extreme illustration to show how serious sin is and how we must do everything necessary to avoid hell: "If your hand causes you to sin, cut it off. It is better for you to enter life crippled than with two hands to go to hell, to the unquenchable fire" (Mark 9:43). Of course, Jesus is not asking you to literally cut your hand off to keep from sinning. Besides, sin is a heart issue, not a hand issue: "Out of the heart come evil thoughts, murder, adultery, sexual immorality, theft, false witness, slander" (Matthew 15:19). However, He is so serious about sin that you also must take sin seriously enough to turn your heart over to Him.

Jesus also described hell as "outer darkness," a place of extreme sadness and torment. "Then the king said to the attendants, 'Bind him hand and foot and cast him into the outer darkness. In that place there will be weeping and gnashing of teeth'" (22:13). The worst thing about this place is the separation from anything good. For all eternity, there is now a chasm between God and everyone in this "outer darkness." It wasn't created for humans. It was created and reserved for the devil and his fallen angels: "Then he will say to those on his left, 'Depart from me, you cursed, into the eternal fire prepared for the devil and his angels'" (25:41).

As heartbreaking as it is, hell will be the eternal home for all those whose name is not found in the Book of Life. "If anyone's name was not found written in the book of life, he was thrown into the lake of fire" (Revelation 20:15). If you live your whole God-given life and exhale your last breath without ever turning to Him as the savior from your sins, you'll miss out on His saving grace, be left out of His Book of Life, and be trapped in an eternity of separation. The irony of life is that you can have a great name here on earth. Your name can be on the sides of buildings and in history books, but the only thing that matters is whether your name is in the Book of Life. Arrogantly, I used to say, "I don't care if I end up in hell, because all my friends will be there anyway. We'll have a heck of a party." How silly I was! There is nothing fun about this place. There is nothing to celebrate there. Nobody to turn to, nobody to talk to, and neverending loneliness. People in hell endure constant suffering and remorse, knowing they had the opportunity to enter heaven with God but turned it down. There is no exit, no way out, no second chance, no redo, no mulligan. There is absolutely no rest in hell. There is no peace there. Anyone who ends up there will not be resting in peace.

As awful as this place sounds, the good news is that the Lord does not desire any human being to be there. He desires all those made in His image to have their names in His Book of Life. This means you. Yes, even you. You may say, "You don't know what I've done. There is no way He wants me in His Book of Life." I am telling you in love that you can't out-sin His power of grace and forgiveness if you turn to Him in faith. His grace is more than sufficient to cover your mistakes. His desire is that none would perish and that all would come to a saving knowledge of truth. "The Lord is not slow to fulfill his promise as some count slowness, but is patient toward you, not wishing that any should perish, but that all should reach repentance" (2 Peter 3:9). "[He] desires all people to be saved and to come to the knowledge of the truth" (1 Timothy 2:4).

So God is calling believers home, and what will home (eternity) be like for those who have their names in the Book of Life? Oh, so much better. Not just better than the awful experience of hell, but also so much better than what earth can offer. The Bible leaves a lot to the imagination when it comes to heaven. Honestly, we know very little about what it will truly be like. Personally, I think God is intentional in withholding so much information from us because it is impossible for us to wrap our little finite minds around the unhindered glory of the literal presence of the infinite. The only thing I can say is that you can take your wonderful, beautiful, all good, most excellent day here on earth and multiply it by a billion, and that still won't even begin to scratch the surface of how glorious and magnificent heaven will be.

That being said, there are a few things that God's Word tells us about heaven. Again, these truths are an encouragement to believers because they give us something to look forward to. They should also give hope to those who have lost loved ones who were followers of Jesus, because they can know on some level what their loved ones are experiencing today.

According to Revelation 7:13–17, we'll be gathered around the throne of Jesus, worshipping Him. He is worthy of this. The worshippers are described as having white robes (see verses 13–14) because they were made pure by the blood of the One they are worshipping. Those whose names are in the Book of Life are able to wear Jesus's robe of purity because He first put on their robes of sin while He hung on the cross. In heaven, we'll never thirst or hunger for anything again (see verse 16). There will be an eternal fullness and completeness. In the physical presence of God, all tears will be wiped away by His tender hand (see verse 17; 21:4). We will be emotionally, physically, mentally, and spiritually perfect. Any defects we felt here on earth will flee before the throne of Jesus. "He will wipe away every tear from their eyes, and death shall be no more, neither shall there be mourning, nor crying, nor pain anymore, for the former things have passed away" (21:4).

In heaven, there won't be any darkness but only beautiful light. There will be no need for the light of the sun because there will be the marvelous light of the Son. "Night will be no more. They will need no light of lamp or sun, for the Lord God will be their light, and they will reign forever and ever" (22:5). The brilliance of the Son of God will be our light for all eternity. Can you imagine what it will be like to stare into the face of Jesus? It's hard to fathom, isn't it? You can look forward to it though. Your Christian loved ones who have died are already experiencing this. Maybe you're thinking, *I can't wait to see Him because I have a lot of questions for Him!* Chances are you won't have those questions anymore, either because they'll all be answered or they will no longer matter once you see Him in all His glory and splendor.

Anything and everything that is seen as a curse here on earth won't have a place in heaven. No cancer. No disease. No addictions. No injustice. No sadness. No loneliness. No fighting. No divorce. No racism. No murder. No rape. No wheelchairs. No handicap parking. This is very personal for our family. Our son from Uganda is in a wheelchair. It brings me such joy to know there will be a day when he is no longer bound to those wheels but rather is running free and whole and perfect in the presence of his perfect savior. "No longer will there be anything accursed, but the throne of God and of the Lamb will be in it, and his servants will worship him" (22:3).

Heaven is a wonderful place where we should all desire to be, knowing that a loving God desires us to be there with Him. There is joy there. There is love there. There is life there. In fact, you could even say that those who are in heaven today are more alive than we are! In that place, they are no longer bound by the same limitations that you and I are still susceptible to. There is rest there. There is peace there because the Prince of Peace is there. If you want to truly rest in peace, then you must know the Prince of Peace.

My friend Dean has this hope for his first wife, Lynne, and his son Elliot. He is not trapped by the lie that God gained an angel each time his loved ones passed away. He has a greater truth that gives him the freedom to continue here on earth, because he is confident that his loved ones were called home by the Prince of Peace to worship Him forever. They are alive. They are complete. They are in the physical presence of Jesus with His face shining upon them. They are truly resting in peace, not as angels, but as sons and daughters of God.

I'd like to share with you an encouraging passage about heaven from Revelation, in which John, the disciple Jesus loved, described it. I'll give him the last word in this chapter:

Then the angel showed me the river of the water of life, bright as crystal, flowing from the throne of God and of the Lamb through the middle of the street of the city; also, on either side of the river, the tree of life with its twelve kinds of fruit, yielding its fruit each month. The leaves of the tree were for the healing of the nations. No longer will there be anything accursed, but the throne of God and of the Lamb will be in it, and his servants will worship him. They will see his face, and his name will be on their foreheads. And night will be no more. They will need no light of lamp or sun, for the Lord God will be their light, and they will reign forever and ever.

And he said to me, "These words are trustworthy and true." (22:1–6)

QUESTIONS FOR COMMON LIE 2

1. Think about someone who has died whose death was really hard for you. How long has it been since he or she passed? What specific times seemed to be the hardest?

2. Why do you think people say things like "God gained another angel" or "RIP"? Do you think these statements are helpful even though the first is not true and the second may not be? Why or why not?

3. What is the most helpful way to care for someone who is grieving the loss of a loved one? What are some helpful things to say? Name a time when someone ministered to you when you were grieving. What specifically did this person say or do that really helped you?

4. When you read the descriptions about heaven and hell in this chapter, what stands out the most to you about each?

5. Read Revelation 21:1–4; 22:1–5. As a Christian, what kind of encouragement does this give you about your eternal home? What do you think people are experiencing right now in heaven? How does this help you as you grieve those who loved Jesus and have passed away?

A Truth to Move Forward With

God is not gaining new angels; rather, He is calling worshippers home.

God Just Wants Me to Be Happy

Greener Grass and
Beautifully Colored Plastic Frogs

My wife, Kasi, and I were in the middle of a crisis. At the time, I was an associate pastor at a church, and Kasi and I were ministering to a married couple from another church. We loved this couple dearly and had known them for many years. The husband was several years older than his wife, and they had married as soon as she graduated from high school. About two years into the marriage, she gave birth to a beautiful baby girl. From the outside, everything looked great—a healthy marriage to cause envy in others.

Then came "the four-year glitch," also known as "the wife decided she no longer wanted to be married." Now twenty-two years old, she informed her husband that she never had an opportunity to—wait for it—"sow her wild oats." They had begun dating when he was twenty-one and she was seventeen. The next thing she knew, she was a wife at eighteen and a mother at twenty. Now she wondered about all the things she felt she'd missed out on. She had a list of regrets: "I never got to party as a single girl. Never went dancing in the clubs. Never got to date other boys and experience all that life had to offer."

This bucket list that she wanted to experience hit him like a ton of bricks. He was shocked by the revelation. Obviously, this was not something she just woke up one day feeling. This thought had been there, possibly for a while, but she'd never communicated it. At some point, a seed of doubt toward their relationship had been planted in her feelings and thoughts. Over time it grew into a giant tree of delusion that would be impossible to cut down because now she was willing to talk only about how she wanted out.

How many times are we convinced there is something better on the other side of the fence? Yeah, cows often follow that same kind of logic. Fish do too. It is just like a fish lured away by a beautifully colored plastic frog on the end of a fishing line—unaware of the hook hidden beneath the plastic. In fact, that is how fishing lures got their name. They *lure* the fish away from their destination, right to a fishing pole held by a hungry fisherman looking for dinner. Cows get their heads stuck in fences, and fish end up hooked and then cooked. Ironic, isn't it? When the pursuit of what you thought would bring you happiness is actually the very thing that robs you of it?

Kasi and I became fully involved in counseling this couple and spent hours praying for them. We tried everything we knew to help save their marriage. I talked and cried with the husband,

and Kasi talked and cried with the wife, who seemed very cold. Kasi would plead, "Think of your family. Think of your baby. And, most importantly, think of your relationship with your heavenly Father." I'll never forget the night Kasi came home after spending a couple of hours with the wife. My beautiful, normally glowing bride looked completely dejected and exhausted. "Shane, it's over. She is leaving him." I was confused and heartbroken for our friends. I had believed there was hope. I replied, "Kasi, what do you mean it's over? Are you certain? How do you know?" I'll never forget Kasi's reply: "I know because of what she said: 'I know that God just wants me to be happy!'"

And there it was. The statement that is always the card people play when they want to justify their actions: "I know God just wants me to be happy!" The statement that is always the excuse people give for ignoring what the Scriptures have to say about their particular breach of ethics: "God just wants me to be happy." The statement that is also a lie.

Here's good question number one: Is our happiness really the determining factor for everything? Is happiness really the greatest good in the world? Statements like "Happy wife, happy life" and "The ultimate goal of life is the pursuit of happiness" have been staples in our society for as long as I can remember. But is that what God's main priority for our lives is—to just be happy?

JOY > HAPPINESS

I've been in ministry for over seventeen years. Unfortunately, I can tell you story after story of people walking away from the truth and teachings of Scripture in order to pursue happiness. Some break a promise, others verbally tear people down, and still others decide not to be married anymore because they found someone else who, unlike their current spouse, "rocks their world." Whatever the situation, they come to a moment of justification and play that card: "At the end of the day, I know God just wants me to be happy."

Now, don't get me wrong. I'm not anti-happy. I'm a big fan of healthy happiness. What I'm talking about is the world's definition of happiness or, even more relevant to each of us, our own view of happiness. The world's idea of happiness is directly tied to circumstances. If our circumstances are favorable, then we're happy. If not, then we're not.

But here's the deal. Our circumstances change all the time. Many of us allow these vacillating circumstances to dictate our happiness. It's an extremely dangerous scenario when outward forces control our inward feelings. If we're pursuing that kind of happiness, we'll end up in a ditch of resentment and regret. It's this elusive lie, like greener pastures or beautifully colored plastic frogs, that lure us away from God's best, eventually hooking us into a fight for our very lives. And we find ourselves stuck or hooked just steps before becoming miserable and depressed (not happy).

Here's good question number two: What if God desires more for us than happiness? Is it possible that in the pursuit of happiness, we're completely missing God Himself? After all, He is the only One who can truly make us happy. Does God have something more in store for you and me than just happiness? Okay, here's the wonderful answer to those good questions. Three little letters: J-O-Y. God desires that you and I experience joy, that settled state of contentment, confidence, and hope that comes only from trusting Him. Sadly though, we often miss it because we're too busy chasing happiness. The truth is, God has a whole lot to say in His Word about this great gift of joy. The word *joy* appears eighty-eight times in the Old Testament and fifty-seven times in the New Testament. Here are three definitive biblical truths that explain why joy is greater than happiness.

Joy Is a Fruit of the Holy Spirit

Joy is the second fruit of the Holy Spirit listed in Galatians 5: "The fruit of the Spirit is love, joy . . ." (verse 22). Out of all the great gift givers in the world, and there are a lot of amazing philanthropists out there, God is the greatest of them all. God is continuously giving His followers His very best—Himself! "This is eternal life, that they know you, the only true God, and Jesus Christ whom you have sent" (John 17:3). This is also the greatest news of the gospel. You get God! You get to know Him, behold Him, experience Him, and have His Spirit live inside you. When God comes to live inside you, you get love, peace, hope, life, and joy.

In the Bible, fruit is a symbol of character. The list of the fruit of the Holy Spirit in Galatians 5 is a list of characteristics that should naturally flow out of Christians' lives when they have God inside them. One of the recurring questions people often struggle with is how to know whether God lives inside them. They ask, "How do I know if I am truly a Christian?" Well, the fruit of the

Holy Spirit should be evident in their lives. This fruit looks different in each of us because each of us is different. And we'll never be perfect in these areas because we are still wrestling against the old sin nature that wants to be the opposite of gentle, kind, loving, and joyful.

However, one of the most distinct markers that the Spirit of God dwells in you is the presence of joy in your life. If you have the Spirit, you will have joy! This is one of the fundamental differences between biblical joy and worldly happiness. We attempt to find happiness from favorable circumstances, but we receive joy only as a gift from the favorable God. Happiness comes and goes as circumstances and feelings change. Joy, however, is here to stay.

Joy Is Not Built on Circumstances but on a Person Named Jesus

Joy will always be wherever Jesus and His Spirit are. Incredible promises are given to the children of God: "I am with you always, to the end of the age" (Matthew 28:20). "I will never leave you nor forsake you" (Hebrews 13:5). These beautiful truths are yet another indication of why joy is truly greater than happiness. Joy is not built on outward circumstances but on Christ dwelling inside believers. If the Spirit of Christ is always inside me and will never leave me, then my joy will never leave me. No matter what I go through, I can have joy because my God is with me. Good days—joy. Bad days—joy. Suffering—joy. When everything goes my way—joy. When nothing goes my way—joy. My joy remains because my Christ remains.

Now, just so we're clear, joy is not always laughing, smiling, and being silly. Don't confuse joy promised in the Bible with upbeat feelings. Remember, feelings come and go, but genuine Christian joy remains. Joy is also not the power of positive thinking or a bubbly, optimistic personality. Suffering and difficulty are very real scenarios that every person must face. Jesus knew suffering all too well. While He was doing good—causing the blind to see, the deaf to hear, and the lame to walk—religious people were conspiring to kill Him. Though He was completely innocent of sin, He took our place on the cross and endured unimaginable suffering and injustice. Yet all the while, He walked, lived, and showed joy. Jesus was joy personified. He was the epitome of contentment, confidence, and hope in who He was and what His heavenly Father had called Him to do. Even in the midst of extreme suffering and injustice, Jesus had—and was—joy!

"C'mon, Shane, of course, He's Jesus! He could do that. He is perfect. I can't do that because I'm not perfect. I'm not Jesus." This is all true. He is Jesus and you're not. However, being a Christian means you have Christ in you. "I have been crucified with Christ. It is no longer I who live, but Christ who lives in me. And the life I now live in the flesh I live by faith in the Son of God, who loved me and gave himself for me" (Galatians 2:20). If it is true that Christ is in you, then it is also true that His joy is in you. Jesus's joy is in you! "These things I have spoken to you, that my joy may be in you, and that your joy may be full" (John 15:11). As long as your focus is on Jesus and His joy inside you, your soul will be satisfied. However, if you take your eyes off Him and begin to chase after the lures of happiness promised by the world, your joy will wane and your soul will become dissatisfied. That sounds too simple, doesn't it? But guess what? It truly is that simple. With Jesus there is joy.

Joy Is a Command from Scripture

Isn't it sad that Christians are often the most miserable people around? Do you know people who walk into the church building on Sundays looking as though they've been sucking on a sour pickle all morning? With a scrunched-up face and a condemning brow, they say, "God is good. All the time. All the time. God is good." To which it takes everything within you not to reply, "Well, would you tell your face that? Because you look absolutely miserable!"

Nothing is more confusing to the world than for God's people to say they have joy in their hearts while they have misery on their faces. The Holy Spirit of God gives all believers this incredible fruit called joy, deep in our souls. Again, this may not cause us to grin from ear to ear, but I do believe it means our countenance should reflect a trust in God's goodness. I love the command from Holy Scripture that specifies when we are to rejoice—*always*. "Rejoice in the Lord always; again I will say, rejoice" (Philippians 4:4). Notice that the verse does not say, "Rejoice when everything is going your way. Rejoice when everything makes sense. Rejoice if you feel like it." But rather, the command is to "rejoice in the Lord always." It's almost as if the writer, the apostle Paul, was saying, "In case you missed it the first time, let me say it one more time— rejoice!" It's not a suggestion. It's not even something to do in response to some good fortune in your life. Rather, this is a command to rejoice at all times, no matter what is going on in your life.

You see, God is pretty serious about joy. The truth is, we're not told to always be happy, but we are commanded to rejoice always.

If you're sick and tired of being sick and tired from the pursuit of happiness, might it be time for you to start resting in joy? Maybe you find yourself in a circumstance that doesn't always make you have happy feelings. Remember, God is with you. If He is with you, then joy is with you too.

When everything makes sense, rejoice. When nothing makes sense, rejoice. When everything is going your way, rejoice. When nothing is going your way, rejoice. When you're rejoicing, you're walking in freedom. You're walking in freedom because you're walking in obedience to your great God!

Only a Real Jesus Brings Real Joy

Kasi and I have five children. Our oldest two are girls, ages twelve and seven, and they both love to play with Play-Doh. They have all the colors and tools necessary to mold, shape, and build anything their vivid imaginations can come up with. Okay, now for a moment of confession. I love to play with them and create as well. It reminds me of my childhood. But my daughters often put me in time-out when I mix the colors to create new ones. It's what I always did as a kid, but they can't stand it. They say, "Daddy, you're ruining it!" To which I humbly reply, "You're not respecting my artistic and creative abilities."

One of the reasons we all liked Play-Doh as children was because we believed we could create anything we wanted. We'd mold, shape, and bend it, and if we didn't like how it was turning out, we could pick everything up, roll it in a ball, and start over.

This same kind of thinking is the reason so many people love to talk about Jesus but don't actually read the Bible. In fact, we've all heard people say such things as "I love Jesus, but I don't like the Bible" and "I have a deep respect for Jesus, but I don't agree with the Bible." This is how people can justify in their minds that God is okay with them breaking clear commandments in Scripture as long as they are happy. As if everything in the Bible is a mere suggestion, as long as you are happy. And the moment you're not happy, feel free to pick everything up, roll it in a ball, and start over as you pursue whatever you need to make you happy. After all, God's greatest purpose for your life is to be happy. Right?

If this is how you believe God operates, then it is possible you are worshipping a Play-Doh Jesus. The main reason you don't have an issue with Jesus but have major problems with what the Bible has to say about certain things is because it's a Jesus you've created by your own imagination. You shape, mold, and bend Him to be what you want Him to be. Then, the very moment that particular Play-Doh Jesus no longer appeases you or makes you happy, you create a different Jesus more to your liking and happiness. The problem with this is that your made-up Jesus will never bring you real freedom, power, or joy because it is not the real Jesus. Only the true Christ from the truth of Scripture can provide real joy.

A real Jesus brings real joy. A fake Jesus brings fake happiness.

The Jesus of the Bible will regularly disrupt our lives, call us to difficult things, and stand in opposition to our personal preferences. He often does the opposite of what we think He should. Let's be honest. His holiness, His demand for us to deny ourselves, and His commandments to love others can all get pretty annoying in our pursuit of happiness. The Jesus of the Bible contests the egoistic fine art of looking out for number one. So our natural inclination is to shape Jesus into something more palatable to our personal opinions and preferences.

Left to our natural devices, we don't want to be created in God's image; we want Him to be created in our image. We don't want Him to be the one in control; we want to be in control. We don't want Him to be the potter and us to be the clay; we want to be the potters and Him to be clay in our hands. We want to shape and mold a god who will care about what we care about. We want to label him as a Republican or Democrat. We want to picture him as white, black, or brown. We want him to be passionate about what we're passionate about. We want him to be angry about what we're angry about. We think he should tolerate what we tolerate. He should be okay with our leaving our spouses if we want to. He should turn a blind eye to the little white lies we must share to get ahead. The god we create understands that we have to cut corners to climb the corporate ladder. In fact, this god exists primarily to make us happy.

If this idea of Jesus is what comes to mind when you worship, pray, sing, lift your hands, give, serve, and live, then I've got to tell you, you're worshipping an idol. You're breaking one of the clearest commandments in all of Scripture, and God won't stand idly by to let it happen for very long. "You shall have no other gods before me. You shall not make for yourself a carved image, or any likeness of anything that is in heaven above, or that is in the earth beneath, or that is in the water under the earth. You shall not bow down to them or serve them, for I the LORD your God am a jealous God" (Exodus 20:3–5). "I am the LORD; that is my name; my glory I give to no other, nor my praise to carved idols" (Isaiah 42:8).

You are worshipping a misrepresentation of the God of the Bible—one to whom you've simply attached the name Jesus. It's sinful because it's not the true Jesus of the Bible that you're worshipping. If you truly love the Jesus of the Bible, then you will also love the Bible that tells us all about Him. "If you love me, you will keep my commandments" (John 14:15). We know nothing about the person and life of Jesus apart from the Holy Scriptures.

Jesus said Himself that we must "worship in spirit and truth" (John 4:24). An accurate view of Him is absolutely necessary for authentic worship and joy! So who is this Jesus of the Bible? According to Colossians, He makes the invisible God visible (see 1:15). He is the firstborn over all creation, which means He is the priority over all that is created (see verse 15). All things were created through Him and for Him, and He is the One who sustains all things (see verses 16–17). He is the head of the church and is the firstborn over death by His resurrection. In all things, He is preeminent (see verse 18). This means that Jesus surpasses all, ranks above all, and deserves first place in everything. We're not the boss. He is. We're not the creator. He is. We're not in control. He is. We're not the potter. He is.

This is the Jesus of Scripture, so let us dive into His Word to discover who He is and not rely on our own made-up views and opinions. "Trust in the LORD with all your heart, and do not lean on your own understanding" (Proverbs 3:5).

In knowing the real Jesus of the Bible, we'll begin to be passionate about what He is passionate about. We'll be angered by what angers Him. We'll tolerate what He tolerates. We'll view things the way He views things. We'll live how He lives. We'll be made joyful by what makes Him joyful.

P.S., Healthy People Know How to Argue

The lie we've shone the light of truth on in this chapter is "God just wants me to be happy." As far as lies go, no doubt that's a big one. But there are several smaller lies that hide in the shadow of that big one, and one of them ties directly into the opening story in this chapter. It's a lie that's often unspoken, an untruth that's all too often simply assumed: "Christians are not supposed to argue." Please accept this short postscript to address this little lie. Kasi and I have learned the benefit of healthy arguing in our marriage, but this P.S. is not just for married couples. When it comes to knowing how to argue, these truths apply to all relationships.

Let's consider, for example, the story of our friends at the beginning of the chapter. This young woman never communicated her struggles, desires, and thoughts until she finally decided to communicate that their relationship was over. It's very likely that bringing up her fear of missing out may have caused some arguments early on in their relationship. However, arguments and communication done well during the journey of a relationship are always better than arguments and communication done poorly as the relationship is falling apart—or, even worse, after it's over. Who knows? As oddly as it sounds, if our friends would have figured out how to argue better, then maybe they'd still be happily married today.

Kasi and I wish this was the only example we could share. Over the years, we've personally seen dozens of friendships and ministry relationships fall apart unnecessarily. Whether it's a relationship with a spouse, children, extended family, friends, co-workers, or peers at school, relationships cannot be built on happy feelings. They have to be built on the firm foundation of Christ. The principles already discussed in this chapter apply to all kinds of relationships. When Jesus is there, joy is there, and when joy is there, contentment is there. If a relationship has joy and contentment, it will last a very, very long time.

When a relationship is dependent on happy feelings, you must desperately do everything you can to keep those feelings intact. If those feelings disappear, then the logic of the lie says it is okay for you to leave to pursue those happy feelings somewhere else. However, if you have joy in your relationships, then you're willing to work hard to keep them together, even if you don't have happy feelings in the moment.

One of the most practical ways to work on your marriage, friendships, or other relationships is by learning how to communicate well. Actually, let's go a step further. Healthy joy in a healthy relationship will allow you to have healthy conflict resolution. Basically, you'll know how to argue well. Every solid relationship requires the art of arguing.

When the phrase *definition of argue* is searched on Google, the following will pop up: "give reasons or cite evidence in support of an idea, action, or theory, typically with the aim of persuading others to share one's view." Is there a way to argue well? You may be thinking, *Wait. Couples are not supposed to argue. After all, isn't every day in marriage like an episode of* The Bachelor, *with helicopter rides, dinner on the beach, and your partner swooning over every word you say?* Unfortunately, reality TV is far from reality, because in real life there are real couples, real friends, and real business relationships that have very real arguments. In fact, people in relationships who say they don't argue typically fall into one of three categories:

1. They're lying.
2. There is a bully. For example, in a marriage, when there is a bully in the house, very little arguing takes place. If one person is strongly dominant and the other is extremely passive, the reason they don't argue is because one is a bully and the other won't ever speak up for himself. He will passively cower while bitterness builds. Eventually he will emotionally and/or physically leave the relationship. Maybe you're in a business partnership that no longer feels like a partnership but rather like a dictatorship. Possibly you're in a friendship that feels much the

same way. You find yourself constantly giving in to your friend's demands and wants without ever being able to communicate your needs within the friendship.

3. Both people have completely given up on having a growing and maturing marriage or relationship. Sadly, in marriage people become functional roommates or partners, letting each other do his or her own thing, or they leave in search of something or someone who will make them happy. At one time, the relationship was easy, natural, and pleasant. However, they've come to realize it would take a lot of work to see the relationship grow and develop, so they give up on it. They just "go along to get along."

However, for those who are willing to tell the truth and admit they argue, are willing to work on growing in communication, and care enough not to fall into the trap of resignation, there is a way to turn disagreements into blessings. Here are five ways to argue well and to make sure that joy *and* happiness remain in your relationships.

You Must Care Enough to Argue

One of the worst feelings in the world is not caring enough to communicate your frustrations, letdowns, and needs. Couples and friends who don't care enough to argue are probably close to giving up. Some of the most difficult statements to hear your spouse or friend say are "It doesn't matter anymore. Do whatever you want. You just do your thing, and I'll do mine." At that point, unless something changes, you can be sure the end is near. Joy has left and is nowhere to be found. Unfortunately, happiness is found only in the times when you are away from each other. In contrast, when you care, it means you want to do whatever it takes to resolve the issue. You're willing to talk, disagree, and then make the necessary changes and sacrifices. Why? Because you love each other and care enough to work it out. Joy in marriages, family relationships, and friendships is that important.

Arguing Well Is About Learning, Not Winning

When you listen to the needs, worries, and frustrations of the other person and learn how to serve each other better, then you have victory in an argument. There are times when you can win a debate and still lose in the long run. Too often we sacrifice the health of our relationship to get in the last word. Relationships are about learning, not winning. When a disagreement takes place with healthy and mature communication, then sacrificial changes are made to show each other beautiful, unconditional love. That is true winning.

A Good Argument Involves Both People Talking and Both People Listening

A good argument is not one person doing all the talking while the other person does all the listening. That is called a lecture. Arguing well is one person talking while the other listens without interrupting. Then it becomes time for the talker to become the listener who avoids interrupting. Also, a good talker communicates with kindness, self-control, and humility. A good listener truly concentrates on what the other person is saying and isn't distracted by thinking about his comeback. He doesn't make it an opportunity to bring up her shortcomings from the past. For example, Sarah says, "John, what you did today really hurt my feelings." John retorts, "Oh really? What about that thing you did to me six weeks ago that really upset me but that I never told you about?" (Because I'm a guy and I don't communicate . . . ever . . . ever . . . ever.)

Arguing Well Is Not Arguing About the Same Things Over and Over Again

If you're continuing to argue about the same things, it means one or both of you are not listening or learning. It's been said that the definition of insanity is doing something over and over again and expecting a different result. For continual growth, there has to be an unwavering effort to change to meet the needs of the other person. When disagreements come, we must communicate, listen, and make the necessary changes.

Argue for the Glory of God

Christian marriages are not about us as individuals or even as couples. Actually, they're about something much bigger than us. According to Ephesians 5, marriage is the visual illustration God has given the world to show Christ's relationship to His bride, the church. "'Therefore a man shall leave his father and mother and hold fast to his wife, and the two shall become one flesh.' This mystery is profound, and I am saying that it refers to Christ and the church" (verses 31–32). Our relationships preach a gospel message to the world; that truth alone makes marriage eternally important. It's necessary for us to ask ourselves this question often: *What kind of message is my marriage preaching to my children, my church, my family, my friends, and a watching world?*

When we understand that our lives, our actions, and our relationships are designed by God to bring Him glory, then our happiness is not the most important thing. God is most important. When He is most important, then we strive to live and love in a way that looks very similar to the way that Jesus lived and loved.

Questions for Common Lie 3

1. What are the differences between the world's definition of happiness and the Bible's definition of joy?

2. It's easy to believe that God's greatest desire for your life is for you to be happy. But if this isn't true, what is God's greatest desire for your life?

3. In what specific time in your life did your circumstances dictate your happiness? How would focusing on joy have been more helpful during that time?

4. In the section of this chapter titled "Only a Real Jesus Brings Real Joy," you read about the idea of a Play-Doh Jesus. What are some ways you've seen people try to shape Jesus into someone different from the way the Bible describes Him? Read John 4:24. What does it mean to worship God "in spirit and truth"?

5. How does learning how to argue in a healthy way help you have joy in your relationships? Name two of the subpoints on arguing that stood out to you the most. How might they help you in the future?

A Truth to Move Forward With

The world's definition of happiness is often dictated by circumstances, but biblical joy is built on a person named Jesus.

I Could Never Forgive That Person

Ozzie's Story

I met Ozzie after delivering a message at a large student conference. The message included topics such as the need for forgiveness, letting go of bitterness, and how holding on to Jesus is better than holding on to grudges. During the time of worship, many students responded to the message, including a pint-size teenage girl with her youth leader by her side. Through tears she told me that she had been holding on to extreme bitterness and an unforgiving attitude toward another person. I thought to myself, *She's maybe sixteen years old, so this is probably over some boy or something even more trivial than that.* I soon found out how ignorant I was!

With tears welling up in her eyes, Ozzie began to share her story:

October 6, 2012, was the worst day of my life. It started out great, probably one of the best mornings I had ever had. I woke up and made myself a delicious breakfast of eggs, toast, and chocolate milk. I helped my mom pick out her outfit for the day—I remember it: an orange shirt, blue jeans, boots, and a pair of gold earrings that I still wear to this day.

We got in the car and began our way down the county road. Half a mile down, my mom and I are laughing a bellyaching laugh, the kind that makes you love life a little bit more. One mile down, we round the corner to see smoke. Nothing out of the ordinary, considering burning trash and brush is a very common practice where I come from. However, when we get closer, I realize the smoke is not from trash or brush but from a house. By the time my brain can register its surroundings, it's too late. I hear a noise that I am very familiar with—a 12-gauge shotgun. Growing up in the country, you get used to the sound of shotguns, typically aimed at birds. But this day the gun was aimed at something else.

Boom. Boom. Boom. Glass is everywhere now, and I have sunk down into my seat, covering my head. My window has been shot out, and I am showered in tiny bits of glass. All I can hear are my own deafening screams. Two more shots are fired. *Boom. Boom.* We aren't on the road anymore. The car isn't moving anymore. *Mom, you're not breathing anymore.* The world around me slows almost to a stop as I see that crimson liquid flowing too fast to stop. I scream for her, but there is no answer. She's gone, and I know I'm next.

I jump out of the car through my shattered window, trying to gather my thoughts, but then there's another *boom*! Then another and another and another. I feel a sting and realize my knee is bleeding. I stop screaming, and the shooting stops. I have to act; it's now or never.

I army-crawl through the brush and make my way to the road. Running to the closest house, which is roughly five hundred yards away, I realize I have only one shoe on, so I kick it off and continue running. I stumble onto the porch and find that the house is locked. I immediately grab a rock, break a window, and climb through to search for a phone. There isn't one. I stand on the front porch and assess my options. After noticing a trail in the woods, I decide to take that route in case the crazed gunman comes after me. Running barefoot through the woods for roughly half a mile only takes me back to the main road, so I begin running close to the edge of the road to be able to easily hide in the woods if he should see me. After another mile of running, I finally get to the next house. My knee has begun to throb unbearably. Now I'm praying and pleading with God that someone will be home. I tell Him that He has gotten me this far, that I know He can save me. But I also tell Him that if it's my time to die, then take me now, and have my mom waiting for me at the gates. I end the prayer by asking Him to let my family know that no matter what happens, it's going to be okay because He is still good and in control!

At the house, I find help and am able to call 911. I tell

the operator that I need an ambulance—a man has killed my mom, I've been shot, and there is a fire. After a short time, sirens ring in the air, and for the first time that day, I cry. I cry tears of joy for being alive and tears of sorrow because my mom isn't. The police officer who arrives first opens his car door and runs to me. I tell him I don't know where the shooter is or if he has followed me. Moments later, I hear the sound of more sirens and am surrounded by emergency personnel. They put me on a gurney. In the ambulance, I hear the paramedic calling in a helicopter for me to be airlifted to a hospital in San Antonio. While we are waiting for the helicopter to arrive, I hear a call on the radio saying, "There's a woman here. She's not breathing, and she appears to have a gunshot wound to the back of the head. She's dead."

The helicopter arrives, and I am about to be loaded into it when I feel arms wrap around me and hear a familiar voice telling me, "I love you, baby girl." It is my dad. He later told me that he saw my blond hair on that gurney, knew it was me, and wasn't letting me get away without talking to me first. The helicopter takes off, and I am on my way to San Antonio. They give me an IV and inject me with some pain medication. After arriving at the hospital, I'm immediately surrounded by what seems like hundreds of hospital workers. They take me to a room to get an MRI.

After the MRI, the doctor tells me I was shot three times and the bullets went all the way through, so there were six holes. I am finally assigned a room, and then I receive a text message from my brother. The gunman who had done all this evil had committed suicide. I was never going to get the opportunity to let this man know that he did not kill me or break me. The months that followed were fine. I mean, yes, I was sad, but I had such a great support system of family and friends around me 24/7. However, when that support group fell away, I became extremely depressed. I felt myself fading and wasn't thinking straight. I wanted to drop out of school and run away. Worst of all, I began blaming God for everything that had happened. I told myself that if He truly loved me, He wouldn't have let this happen to me and my family. My hatred for the man who did this had turned toward God, and honestly, I was beginning to have thoughts of suicide. I was harboring anger, bitterness, and unforgiveness. There was no way I was ever going to forgive God or the gunman for taking my mom away from me and wounding me physically and emotionally. I was a complete wreck and was ready to give up.

The Rest of the Story

After hearing her story, I stood speechless. I'd never heard anything like it in my life. Bible college and seminary did not teach me how to respond to something like this. I felt as if the air had been completely punched out of me. As I attempted to speak, my voice cracked and changed multiple pitches. It sounded like I was going through puberty all over again. I stumbled over my words, but I managed to get out, "Um, well, first of all, wow! I can't begin to imagine what you're feeling or thinking. I'm not going to disrespect you by pretending that I know what you've been through. I can see why you couldn't forgive . . ." And that is when she interrupted me, continuing with the rest of her story.

> Let me finish what I am here to tell you. I was struggling with bitterness and unforgiveness, but tonight you were speaking to us about our forgiveness from the Lord, our call to forgive others, and the need to let go of bitterness. I knew I needed to forgive the man who gunned down my mom and tried to kill me as well. Holding a grudge against him was only harming me. So tonight I asked God to forgive me for holding on to this grudge against Him and the man who killed my mother. As soon as I chose forgiveness, it felt like a load of bricks had been lifted off my chest. Jesus had forgiven me of my sins that nailed Him to the cross, and because of that, I knew I could finally and truly forgive the man who murdered my mom. I no longer have to carry around the burden of bitterness, because I left that weight at the foot of the cross this very night.
>
> I can now walk in the freedom of forgiveness. This includes my own forgiveness, while also choosing to forgive others. I see now that going through this horrifying event has molded me into the person I am today. I do, however, suffer from PTSD. At random times I have

flashbacks of what happened that day; certain smells cause flashbacks; gunshots, fireworks, and other unexpected noises frighten me; and sometimes even hearing sirens makes my heart race. Obviously, I would have planned things differently, but I believe that the Lord is going to use this to teach me so much more about valuing every single breath, forgiveness, courage, and how to never take anything in my life for granted. Because of Jesus, I am stronger than I ever thought possible, and my relationship with Him is stronger than ever. I choose forgiveness because my great God has chosen to forgive me.

Okay. Full stop. Absolutely amazing, right? I remember telling her that was one of the most powerful stories I had ever heard. Ozzie, her youth leader, and I continued to talk for about another fifteen minutes. Then I prayed for her and asked her to pray for me.

But I have to be honest. When I got back to my hotel room that night, I was a little skeptical. So I googled the story to check its validity, and sure enough, everything she said was true and had been covered in the news. Then, deep conviction began to set in as I started thinking about the unforgiveness and bitterness I was holding on to. Nothing that had ever happened to me was even in the same universe as what happened to Ozzie. If God had reminded her of the grace in her life through my message, ironically, He was now reminding me, through her story, of things that I needed to let go. "You hypocrite, first take the log out of your own eye, and then you will see clearly to take the speck out of your brother's eye" (Matthew 7:5).

Naturally, people don't like to (and, frankly, don't want to) forgive. We want to hold on to bitterness because we think, *If I forgive the people who have hurt me, then I'm condoning their actions. I'm saying what they did is okay.* But that is not true at all. God is the judge, and He will judge appropriately. Bitterness, lack of forgiveness, and grudges often harm the one holding on to them the most. However, when we forgive, we essentially say, *You can't destroy me, end me, or hinder me any longer, because my God heals. He is better than bitterness.* It also shows the world that we truly understand how much God has forgiven us. It's a hard question to ask yourself: *Is this going to make me bitter, or is it going to make me better?* And the answer is, "It can't be both."

Plus, let's be honest. Most of our unforgiveness and bitterness stem from some really silly and trivial situations. However, some stories, such as Ozzie's, involve true victims. In these kinds of stories, forgiveness can come only from God because they take a God-sized forgiveness. And it's in stories like these that we can see ourselves and our own situations more clearly. If Ozzie can forgive a man who murdered her mother, can't I forgive the silly and trivial situations in my own life?

Even as I write this, images of people are popping up in my mind, reminding me of times when I allowed bitterness to creep into my soul over situations that really were not that big a deal. In my years of being a leader, pastor, and communicator, my pride has been bruised at times because people said something negative about how I spoke or taught. They just didn't like what I was doing. They'd say things such as, "Shane's preaching is not what I am used to. I think I'd prefer another pastor." At one time, someone made the comment, "I wish Shane would focus more on serving the community," while another person said, "I hope Shane will eventually focus more on the church and stop focusing on the community so much."

Notice these people weren't saying they didn't like me; rather, they just didn't like something I was doing or not doing. In fact, most of the time it had nothing at all to do with me personally. They just preferred a different style or a different approach. But, as unhealthy and silly as it was, I took these comments like arrows straight to my heart. They were a shot to my pride. A blow to my ego. Sometimes I'd try to adjust and attempt to perform in a way that would gain their approval. The majority of the time, I took it so personally that I'd allow the hurt from my bruised ego to fester. The feelings were suppressed on the inside and eventually turned into bitterness. It was immaturity at its finest and bitterness at its worst, all directed toward people who had no clue I was upset with them. They did nothing wrong, and initially I did nothing wrong; however, what I allowed the situation to turn into—deep, deep inside me—was extremely wrong. It was silly. It was trivial. It was destructive. There had to be a moment of letting go. Reflecting on Ozzie's story has continued to encourage and challenge me in the best of ways.

How about you? Are you holding on to bitterness and grudges? Is it possible you are trapped by the lie that you could never forgive that person? And are you stuffing down all those unhealthy feelings on the inside?

Most of the time, the reason we're not able to walk in freedom by setting aside our bitterness and unforgiveness is because we believe some very destructive myths about forgiveness. These myths often serve as barriers between us and the victory we so desperately need. It's imperative that we identify what they are so we can avoid them on our journey to freedom through forgiveness.

Forgiveness Lies

One of the scariest verses in all of Scripture has to be Matthew 6:14–15, where Jesus said, "If you forgive others their trespasses, your heavenly Father will also forgive you, but if you do not forgive others their trespasses, neither will your Father forgive your trespasses." This is one of those verses that you'll never see on a Christian T-shirt, coffee mug, or desktop screen saver with roses in the background. The reason this is not a popular verse is that it digs deep into the uncomfortable areas of our lives and deals with some difficult actions on our part. It teaches us that if we're going to be recipients of God's grace, then we must give grace to others. Jesus gives the challenge that if we don't forgive others, it may be proof that we've never truly received God's forgiveness ourselves. Or, in a positively glorious implication, He is teaching us that the most practical way to show the world that we understand forgiveness in our own lives is by showing that we know how to forgive.

I don't agree with everything author Anne Lamott says, but when she speaks about forgiveness, she's right on target:

> I really believe that earth is forgiveness school. . . . For me, it all begins with the hardest work of all, of being so crazily

imperfect, and so sensitive and thin-skinned, and looking the way I look instead of like Cate Blanchett, which is disappointing. And all of the things we internalize in our younger years that other people might have said or hinted or even bullied us for.

To forgive someone is the hardest work we do. I've had to be disciplined about it. . . .

Not forgiving makes you toxic. And then you really have very little to offer your family or the world or your audience, because you're faking it.*

Earth is forgiveness school? Man, she's right. And her comment that "not forgiving makes you toxic"? I know that all too well from personal experience. So, yes, if forgiveness really is that important, then knowing the difference between forgiveness truths and forgiveness lies can make a world of difference in your life and the lives of those around you. Let's identify some of the lies about forgiveness and be sure to call them what they are—lies.

Forgiveness Means You Have to Forget

Unfortunately, this is completely unrealistic for most people and most situations. We don't have a neuralyzer from the movie *Men in Black* that causes our memories to be erased if we look into its flash. Memories are very real, especially if they're wrapped in hurt and letdowns. They may always be there. However, we have the

---

* Anne Lamott, Facebook, December 2, 2014, www.facebook.com/AnneLamott
  /posts/593723490757298.

wonderful opportunity of operating in a lifestyle that says, *I have not been able to forget. I remember it very well, and yet by God's grace I still choose to forgive.* This shows others the ultimate picture of grace. It's exactly what God did for us. He knew our sin and what it would cost Him (His Son), yet He still chose the route of forgiveness.

> He was pierced for our transgressions;
>> he was crushed for our iniquities;
> upon him was the chastisement that brought us peace,
>> and with his wounds we are healed.
> All we like sheep have gone astray;
>> we have turned—every one—to his own way;
> and the LORD has laid on him
>> the iniquity of us all. (Isaiah 53:5–6)

Forgiveness Means You're Condoning the Actions of Others

If we're honest with ourselves, this is what holds us back the most when it comes to extending grace and forgiveness. Many times we feel that choosing to forgive is saying that what a particular person did to us was okay. However, this is a lie. Forgiveness is trusting God to be the ultimate and perfect judge. He knows how to settle our disputes much better than we do. After all, He, not us, is the expert at dealing with sinners and sinful actions. Let's not forget how He has perfectly dealt with our sinful actions toward others. "The heavens declare his righteousness, for God himself is judge! *Selah*" (Psalm 50:6).

Personally, I think it's very intentional that the writer of this psalm placed *Selah* right after the promise that God is judge. Most Bible scholars have taken *Selah* to be a pause or a break or to mean forever. How fitting, right? You're not to be judge, because there is room for only one judge in the courtroom of life. All rise for the honorable, righteous Judge, also known as the perfect God who judges everything perfectly. Now you can pause, take a break, and breathe, because God knows your situation and will perfectly judge it.

Forgiveness Means You Have to Be a Doormat

Often we're terrified to forgive because we're scared to be hurt over and over again. There is only one person to blame in this, and ironically, it's not the one who is stepping on us. No, it is the one who keeps lying down as a doormat to be stepped on. Forgiveness doesn't mean I have to subject myself to being continually abused and used. In fact, I could be guilty of enabling others if I'm their doormat, and this is no help to them. Forgiveness means I'm going to protect myself and free myself from others by not carrying with me the bitterness caused by them. This gives ultrameek Christians permission to be strong and assertive when they need to, while still having a forgiving heart. "Be watchful, stand firm in the faith, act like men, be strong" (1 Corinthians 16:13). This is an incredible reminder for us to be aware of our surroundings, stand with confidence, and be strong in our trust in Christ. The "act like men" part doesn't neglect over half of the world's population. What does it mean? Be mature. It's time to grow up. Be an adult. Stand up for yourself.

Forgiveness Means You Have to Be Close Friends Again

Take a moment to think about how many close friends you *used* to have, but now those relationships are far from close friendships. Yes, the key word here is *used*. There could be various reasons for this. Life changes, such as moving locations or the shifting of interests, may take your relationship in a different direction. Other times you might lose a friend over something really, really minor—maybe even silly. In this scenario, a simple phone call or face-to-face conversation could help you gain your good friend back.

Then there are those unique circumstances in which you don't need to be friends anymore. Sometimes the healthiest thing for two people is distance. We're commanded by Scripture to forgive others, love others, and be kind to others; however, nowhere in Scripture are we commanded to be friends with everyone. Sometimes the best way to forgive someone else is to stay very far away. "Behold, I am sending you out as sheep in the midst of wolves, so be wise as serpents and innocent as doves" (Matthew 10:16). For the most part, snakes intentionally stay away from danger and can easily maneuver around barriers. Doves are innocent, meek, and graceful. Be wise and full of grace. Sometimes being wise and graceful calls you to remove yourself from a harmful situation.

Forgiveness Comes from an Apology

Often we think that the two words *I'm sorry* are supposed to heal all wounds. However, true forgiveness can't come from hearing a pithy statement but rather comes from an all-powerful God. God must first forgive the one who is doing the forgiving. Then the forgiving one must truly experience and enjoy God's forgiveness for himself. "Be kind to one another, tenderhearted, forgiving one another, as God in Christ forgave you" (Ephesians 4:32). Then and only then will the person offering forgiveness be in a healthy place to allow God to grant forgiveness through him to the transgressor. In short, forgiveness comes from God, not us. Once you experience the beautiful taste of grace and forgiveness in your own life, you are called to extend grace and forgiveness to others, whether they say "I'm sorry" or not.

Forgiveness Is Based on the Actions of Others

People often say, "I will forgive that person when she asks me for it and starts doing things to deserve my forgiveness." However, this is a lie because as Christians, we're commanded to forgive, whether someone asks for it or not. Victory in this area will come from obedience to God, not from a reaction to other people's actions. Remember, grace is giving something to others even when they don't deserve it. They may never apologize or do as they should. Never forget, we forgive primarily out of obedience to God and for the freedoms we will experience through letting go of bitterness. "See to it that no one fails to obtain the grace of God; that no 'root of bitterness' springs up and causes trouble, and by it many become defiled" (Hebrews 12:15).

Forgiveness Is Easy

Forgiveness is not easy. It's also not difficult. Forgiveness is actually impossible. In our natural state, we want to hold on to unforgiveness, bitterness, and anger because on some level it makes us feel in control. We want the person who hurt us to hurt like we have. We simply can't change these feelings on our own. However, the good news is that we have a God who makes the impossible possible. "For nothing will be impossible with God" (Luke 1:37). Ultimately, forgiveness is an act of faith in a God who can and will do what we cannot do on our own.

Although there are many lies about forgiveness, there is only one truth. The truth is that bitterness, unforgiveness, and anger are a heavy and miserable load to carry. I think about the word Lamott used: "toxic." And then I think about Ozzie's powerful, life-changing words to me: "I choose forgiveness because my great God has chosen to forgive me."

Healthy Responses to Criticism

But what about those times that are not on the level of Ozzie's story, those situations that honestly are trivial and possibly even silly? If I'm honest (and I try to be), that's the majority of situations I find myself in. I'm sensitive. I wear my feelings on my sleeve, which makes it easy for someone to hurt them. If I had to boil down all the situations in which I've been hurt, many have involved criticism.

In life, there are three things we can't avoid: death, taxes, and criticism. From the suburbs of Texas to the urban areas of New York to the jungles of the Congo to the mountains of Nepal, people are desperately trying to figure out how to respond to criticism. It can cause a lot of pain, destroy relationships, and be a petri dish in which unforgiveness and bitterness are allowed to grow into a life-threatening disease.

Criticism. We receive it, we despise it, we can't avoid it, and most of the time it hits us when we least expect it. It can come from all sorts of people—spouses, bosses, friends, enemies, church members, and complete strangers. Although we can't control how criticism comes our way, we can control how we respond to it. I have a strategy I call the COT response. Usually a cot is thought of as a portable bed used for lying down. However, COT allows people to respond to criticism in a healthy way and not lie down in defeat, doubt, or discouragement.

When criticism comes your way, ask yourself, *Do I need to chuck it (C), own it (O), or test it (T)?* Let me briefly elaborate on each one.

Do I Need to Chuck It?

One thing you must never forget as a Christian is that you are in the middle of a spiritual war. You're not wrestling "against flesh and blood, but against the rulers, against the authorities, against the cosmic powers over this present darkness, against the spiritual forces of evil in the heavenly places" (Ephesians 6:12). You may not ultimately be fighting against flesh and blood, but the Enemy sure does use the flesh of red-blooded people to destroy you and discourage you from following the will of God. Yes, God is alive, but so is the devil. You can be sure that wherever God is moving, Satan will be attacking. It's in moments like these that you need to discern the scheming of the Enemy through criticism and chuck it! "Be sober-minded; be watchful. Your adversary the devil prowls around like a roaring lion, seeking someone to devour" (1 Peter 5:8). Don't be devoured by criticism.

I've had to practice this principle multiple times in my life, especially as a pastor and communicator. Plenty of people have wanted me to change who I am, my style of communicating, and my strategy of leadership. Some have given helpful suggestions, but others have proved to want nothing more than to change who I am to fit their preferences. In these moments, you have to be honest with who God has created you to be and not try to become what others want you to be to fit their selfish agendas. On more than one occasion, I've had to chuck criticism.

Do I Need to Own It?

Let's face it. Some of the most insecure people in the world are Christians, especially Christian leaders. We tend to wear our hearts on the outside of our chests. We don't enjoy being challenged, questioned, or criticized. However, we all need to own up to a very important truth every single day—we are not perfect! Let's be honest: we all make mistakes. A lot of them! There are moments in your life when you're not operating in the Spirit but rather are walking in the flesh and making a mess of things. The Lord says you must constantly "consider your ways" (Haggai 1:7). There are moments when you flat out need to own it because it's time to consider your ways and then change your ways. You cannot arrogantly assume that every word of criticism is coming from someone being used by the Enemy. In fact, sometimes those challenging statements are coming from someone being used by God because you needed to hear them! In these moments, if you begin to allow roots of bitterness to set in, it is completely your fault. That's the time to turn to God and ask Him to forgive you for being too prideful to receive correction in love.

Embarrassingly, I can share this with you only because I've had to do this often. What communicates love to my wife the loudest is my spending quality time with her. At about year six of our marriage, she had a good old-fashioned "come to Jesus" talk with me. A "come to Jesus" talk is how I like to refer to a direct conversation which, at the end of it, either you come to Jesus in repentance and change what is needed or you may end up going to see Jesus soon and very soon. My definition of quality time had been us sitting in the same room together watching football with me sometimes dozing off in my chair. However, her definition of quality time looked nothing like that. It was the television off, us facing each other, and talking. I needed to hear that. It was time to make the necessary changes for the health and vitality of our marriage. My ministry to the world involved communicating, but I had stopped communicating with the most important person in the world to me—my wife. And I had to own that.

Do I Need to Test It?

Sometimes you'll know immediately that someone is operating in the flesh and/or being used by the Enemy to speak to you with ill intentions. Other times you'll be convicted by the Holy Spirit that you're in the wrong. You have the wrong attitude or the wrong motivation, and God showed you grace by speaking to you through someone else. However, most of the time it is not going to be so easy to know how you should respond to criticism. Should you chuck it or own it? In those moments when it's not so clear, what should you do? I say test it.

There are three ways to do this. When criticism comes your way, the first thing you should do is take it to God in prayer. Ask Him to reveal truth in those critical moments, to bring comfort when you need protection from the Enemy, and to convict you when people need protection from you. Second, test it with Scripture. God is not going to speak through someone in a way that is contrary to His Word. Third, seek wise counsel. People you love and trust will be able to protect you from harmful words but will also be able to tell you when you're in the wrong and need to change. It's important to have people in your life whom you trust to give you wise counsel. People who love you, want the best for you, and are not scared to say difficult things to you. I have three people like that whom I tell just about everything to. Their counsel has been one of the most valuable things in my life. They have made my goal of pursuing a life that is pleasing to the Lord and a blessing to others much more attainable. I could not imagine navigating this life without them. So when in doubt, test it and pay close attention to the way God speaks.

Be Like Ozzie

Through a gracious God who granted Ozzie victory over unforgiveness and bitterness, she has seen her tragedy in a very uncommon light. She believes that her story did not sneak up on the

Lord. She now realizes that despite the nightmare she lived through, there was a new morning coming. Ozzie believes that God allowed this tragedy to happen in her life so that out of it she can minister to others. I know that in a book about avoiding clichés, this sounds cliché, but it's true: difficulties will either make you *bitter* or make you *better*.

Not long ago, I checked in on Ozzie and she told me,

> Lately, I've been given opportunities to share my story by speaking to others. I get to speak about how the Lord has used this in my life to teach me so much about forgiveness— His forgiveness toward me and my forgiveness toward others, even the man who murdered my mom. It's hard for the world to understand, but I feel so blessed to have the life that I have today. October 6, 2012, was by far the worst day of my life. But it most certainly will not be the day that breaks me or causes me to lose my faith. It was just an extremely difficult day in the joy-filled journey that God has prepared for me.

The first time I heard Ozzie's story, it left me speechless. I had the same response when she gave me that recent update. I was speechless again. If anyone deserves to be bitter and angry or harbor unforgiveness, it is Ozzie. However, that is not her choice. She chose to see her own grievous sin toward a God who loves her and forgives her anyway. Daily, she chooses to follow an amazing God who dishes out amazing grace. She chooses to worship a God who can weave our test into a testimony and our mess into a message.

She chooses freedom. She chooses forgiveness. She chooses to believe the truths of Scripture and not the lies of her feelings. To the lie "I'll never be able to forgive that person," Ozzie said, "No. Greater is He who is within me than He who is in the world. So I choose to forgive." And she did.

Be like Ozzie.

QUESTIONS FOR COMMON LIE 4

1. What are some initial thoughts that came to mind when reading Ozzie's story? How does her story affect the way you view the people who have hurt you?

2. Think of someone who has hurt you. How has that story turned out? Have you forgiven this person? Are you still in the process of forgiveness? Do you feel as though forgiveness is unattainable in this situation? If so, what makes you say that?

3. From the section of this chapter titled "Forgiveness Lies," what are some of the lies you have believed about forgiveness? How have they held you back in your journey of forgiveness? How could this chapter's truth specifically help you in the future?

4. Name the three responses from the section titled "Healthy Responses to Criticism." Which one of these do you naturally use the most? Why? Which one do you need to get better at?

5. Take time to list two things God has forgiven you for. Did you feel you deserved that forgiveness? Since you have received the grace and forgiveness of God, whom do you need to extend grace and forgiveness to today?

A Truth to Move Forward With

If I am going to be a receiver of forgiveness, then I must be a giver of forgiveness.

Follow Your Heart

A Poisoned Apple?

It was late spring 2005, and all across America graduation ceremonies were underway. You know what those look like; they all have three pieces in common: caps and gowns, proud families in attendance, and commencement speakers giving their speeches. At Stanford University in June 2005, that last piece was quite impressive, a speech delivered by none other than the man behind Apple computers, Steve Jobs. One fun fact is that Jobs never graduated from college. Anyway, Steve Jobs stood before the graduates and their families and gave a rousing speech. Near the conclusion were these two paragraphs, which have become almost like scripture in the minds of some people:

> No one wants to die. Even people who want to go to heaven don't want to die to get there. And yet death is the destination we all share. No one has ever escaped it. And

that is as it should be, because Death is very likely the single best invention of Life. It is Life's change agent. It clears out the old to make way for the new. Right now the new is you, but someday not too long from now, you will gradually become the old and be cleared away. Sorry to be so dramatic, but it is quite true.

Your time is limited, so don't waste it living someone else's life. Don't be trapped by dogma—which is living with the results of other people's thinking. Don't let the noise of others' opinions drown out your own inner voice. And most important, have the courage to follow your heart and intuition. They somehow already know what you truly want to become. Everything else is secondary.*

It was as if Jobs reached out with an actual apple for every graduate there and said, "Eat this." And they did, every bite. I have to admit, there's some truth in there. But there's also a lie that has poisoned, and continues to poison, the minds of the smart, the not so smart, and everyone else in between. He prefaced it with the phrase "and most important," and then he gave it to them, one of the oldest lies in the book: "Follow your heart."

Why Following Your Heart Is a Really Bad Idea

"Follow your heart." How many times have we been handed this as a piece of good advice? If I had a dime for every time I've heard

---

* Steve Jobs, commencement address, Stanford University, June 12, 2005, https://news
.stanford.edu/2005/06/14/jobs-061505/.

it, I'd have a lot of dimes. In fact, this cliché comes with its own line of merchandise—shirts, posters, coffee mugs, you name it.

In seeking out help, wisdom, and guidance, we speak to loved ones, people we look up to and respect, or even professional counselors, and many of these conversations end with the same sort of counsel: "At the end of the day, you just need to do what your heart tells you." As though your heart is this infallible guide inside you that will never lead you astray. This advice makes you believe that your heart has a preprogrammed GPS that will always lead you in the right direction, will never get you lost, will thump inside you when you're about to make a really bad decision, and will leap with joy to let you know when you're about to make a great decision. Wow! That sounds nice, doesn't it? If only it were true.

In reality, this is a secular saying that reads like a fortune cookie in a bad Chinese buffet restaurant. Culture tells us this is the ultimate determining factor in making decisions: "What is your heart telling you to do?" Unfortunately, this statement has also made its way into the church's vernacular, and like many of the other common lies from which we need to find freedom, this one is completely unbiblical. Not only is this lie unbiblical, but it is also really, really bad advice.

Now, in no way do I believe this cliché is given with ill intent. In fact, I believe wholeheartedly that well-meaning people give this advice because they believe it's true, helpful, and wise. Perhaps these same people don't know what else to say. However, if this is how we're ultimately going to make life-altering decisions about topics such as our career path, which school to attend, relationships, and where to live, shouldn't we consider what this overly used statement really means? What does it mean to "follow your heart"?

First of all, we must ask ourselves, What is the heart?

The Scriptures were written primarily to people of Greek and Hebrew cultures. To truly understand the heart and the biblical teachings regarding it, we must see them through the eyes of the authors instead of our twenty-first-century Western lens. To us the heart is a muscle, protected by our rib cage, that pumps blood through our veins to the rest of the body. However, thousands of years ago in different cultures, the heart meant something significantly different.

The word *heart* in Hebrew is *lebab* or *leb* and in Greek is *kardia*. Collectively, the words are used over three hundred times throughout the Bible, making it the most commonly used term in Scripture in reference to human functionality. Interestingly, the Greek word *kardia* is where we get the English word *cardiologist,* which we know to be a heart doctor. The word carries with it the meaning and belief that the heart is the hub of our emotions, our desire producer, and the center of our being. Plain and simple, the heart represents the locus of our feelings, desires, and emotions.

So if we break down the cliché "Follow your heart," it would go something like this:

Follow: Implies that something/someone is going to lead me.

Your heart: According to this statement, what's going to lead me is my heart. However (now that I properly understand the real meaning of the word *heart*), what I am saying is, "My feelings, desires, and emotions are going to be my guide."

Do you see where this leads? This statement's no longer just a well-meaning cliché or a cute, glittery T-shirt. It is actually harmful advice and would be a really dumb idea to live out practically. My guide, leader, and boss are going to be my feelings, desires, and emotions? No, thank you! Besides the Lord, no one knows me better than I do. I know me! My feelings, desires, and emotions change all the time. They can change with a phone call, a word of criticism, or a traffic jam. Honestly, I'm a tad bit of an emotional roller coaster with the ups, downs, and occasional loops and twists. I'm not sure that roller-coaster-polar is a clinical diagnosis, but I tend to be up when everything is going my way, when people are patting me on the back, and when my family is doing okay. However, I can be down when it seems as though the harder I try the more I mess up, when a lot of criticism is coming my way, or when I know my family is suffering. This is why I identify with the psalms and their writers so much. In one psalm, the author wrote, "To you I lift up my eyes, O you who are enthroned in the heavens!" (123:1). In another, "I am weary with my crying out; my throat is parched. My eyes grow dim with waiting for my God" (69:3). I don't know about you, but I connect with that—up and down, hot and cold, spiritually high and spiritually low.

This is why I cannot follow my feelings, desires, and emotions. If I were to follow them, I'd be all over the map with my decisions. Unfortunately, if we are honest with ourselves, many Christians are just that—all over the map; completely lost in direction, stability, and functionality in their daily lives.

As mentioned earlier, the Bible has a lot to say about the heart, and most of what it says carries a negative connotation. For example, the prophet Jeremiah wrote this: "The heart is deceitful above all things, and desperately sick; who can understand it?" (Jeremiah 17:9). The greatest Bible teacher of all, Jesus, also pointed out the fallen condition of our hearts: "From within, out of the heart of man, come evil thoughts, sexual immorality, theft, murder, adultery, coveting, wickedness, deceit, sensuality, envy, slander, pride, foolishness. All these evil things come from within, and they defile a person" (Mark 7:21–23). Basically, the most vile and disgusting acts a human being can be involved with begin in the heart.

If we believe the teachings of Jeremiah and Jesus concerning the heart, then we should seriously consider this question: If a person was described with these characteristics, would you sign up to follow him? Think about this scenario:

I say to you, "I have a person I would like to introduce you to. In fact, I believe this person could be a great mentor for you. He should be your leader and guide, and you should do whatever he tells you to do. Follow him. Trust him. Always ask, 'What is he telling me to do?'"

You reply, "Wow! If I'm going to put this much trust in this person, then I should probably know something about him. Can you describe him for me?"

I respond, "Sure! I'd be happy to. He is deceitful above all things and is desperately sick. He also produces evil thoughts, has a tendency toward sexual immorality, likes to steal and kill, commits adultery, covets, and is wicked, envious, slanderous, and prideful. To top it all off, he is also foolish!"

More than likely you reply, "Are you kidding? What's wrong with you? Are you trying to get me killed? Do you think I'm a fool? I'd never follow someone like that!"

And of course you wouldn't follow, trust, or choose to be influenced by someone like that. No sane person would. Why, then, would you ever follow your heart, described exactly the same way by the One who created it and knows it best?

I could fill the pages of this book with examples of blindly following my heart into bad decision after bad decision. However, probably none of my examples are more painful and destructive than the numerous times I followed my heart into unhealthy relationships.

I was in sixth grade the first time I fell in love. I'm not sure I understood what that even meant at the time, although it sure felt like love. To protect the girl's identity, we'll call her Bertha. (Obviously this is not even close to her real name. However, I did grow up way, way outside the city in an area some people affectionately call the boondocks or the boonies. So it's not at all out of the realm of possibility that her name would be Bertha. But I digress. It's not.) I desperately wanted her to be my

girlfriend, so I decided to write her a love letter. This is exactly
what I wrote:

> *Bertha,*
>> *Will you go with me? Circle*
>
>> *YES or NO*
>
>> *Love,*
>> *Shane "The Stud Muffin" Pruitt*

Yes, sadly, I put "The Stud Muffin." I, in all my twelve-year-
old manliness, referred to myself as a stud muffin. Only by some
kind of cosmic accident did she circle yes.

And we were in love! The playground by the monkey bars was
our special spot. We were planning our wedding day and naming
our future kids. I even attempted to have my first girlfriend and
my first kiss all in one day. She consumed my thoughts and feelings. Every beat of my heart was for her. And guess what? We were
a couple for five whole days. In the sixth grade, that is a long-term
relationship!

Then Bertha wrote me a note:

> *Shane,*
>> *I do not want to go with you any longer. We are*
>> *breaking up.*
>
>> *Bertha*
>
>> *P.S. You are not a stud muffin!*

It was over. All over. I was devastated. My heart was broken, and my feelings were shattered. As embarrassing as it is to admit now, I believed my life was over at twelve years old. My sixth grade career was over. I thought, *I shall never love again. I will never follow my heart again.* I felt that way for three whole class periods, until a seventh-grade girl asked me to be her boyfriend.

I'm back, baby! An older woman!

This was innocent and fun at the time, but it was also where it all began—a constant cycle of following my heart into relationship after relationship. My feelings led me to believe that each new relationship was "the one." Even worse, I believed I always had to be with someone. If I wasn't in a relationship, I wasn't complete. All throughout junior high this was the case. It continued into high school, but in my sophomore year I upped the stakes. Sex entered the picture. For the rest of high school and into college, until I was twenty-one, I bounced from relationship to relationship while giving myself away to any girl who would let me. It was ugly. Honestly, I didn't care about the relationships any longer. I just wanted to feel good. Feel like a man. I was a slave to my feelings, and I used girls to get the feelings I desired. Then, when I got bored, my heart would lead me to the next girl.

My heart led me to believe I needed someone else to make me complete, even if it was only for a few minutes. My heart made me feel that love was found in the back seat of a car. Little did I know at the time that I was losing pieces of my heart all over Central Texas.

Eventually things changed. But it wasn't until I stopped following my heart and began to follow Jesus. He showed me that

He is the only One who can make me complete. Thank God I began following Him, because He led me right to a green-eyed girl named Kasi, who one day said "Yes!" when I asked her to marry me.

The Need for a Heart Transplant

Why are our hearts in that kind of condition? Why are they constantly attacking us? Did God create our hearts to be this way?

In the first three chapters of Genesis, we read the story of creation. In the beginning was God. On day one, He was already there; He always has been. Even when there was nothing, there was God. This God is a creative God. And what do creators do? They create. So this creative God began to create. In chapter 1, we find a detailed account of the six days of creation. Whether those days represent literal twenty-four-hour days or other time periods is debatable and frankly not the point of the first part of Genesis. The overarching theme of Genesis 1 is that God is creative and has the power to create something from nothing. He took special care in creating humanity in His own image. Also, God shows us a beautiful model of how He operates in His creation. Most of us miss this little detail about what He was doing in the first chapters of Genesis.

God created, and then He filled His creation. Think about it. God created space and then filled it with stars and galaxies. He created the oceans and then filled them with marine life. He created the sky and then filled it with birds. He created the land and then filled it with every creeping thing. He created mankind and then filled them with His breath of life.

God fills what He creates. Wow! What an incredibly creative, powerful, and loving God He is. You can see God's care and compassion specifically in how He created humanity. Moses, the human author of Genesis, used the name Elohim for God, which means "the Strong One." This all-powerful One intentionally made humankind as the crowning jewel of all His creation. Elohim made man in His own image. In Latin, it's the term *Imago Dei,* which means we're made in the image and likeness of God.

Libraries could be filled with volumes of books describing what it means for us to be made in the image of God. However, a simple definition of *Imago Dei* is that out of all creation—the moons, stars, mountains, and your pet Chihuahua—nothing resembles God more than humanity does. Now, let's get this straight. We're not God, we're not equivalent to God, nor should we worship ourselves as gods. What it means is that we are mirrors that should reflect God's image and glory more than anything else in the world. When the rest of creation looks at humanity, they should be able to see God's greatness.

This fact alone sets humankind apart from the rest of creation. We're different. We're valuable. We matter because the One whose image we bear matters. His eternal value is placed upon us, and this truth makes us priceless works of art. You and I are the greatest masterpieces of the greatest Artist of all time! As God's masterpieces, we're not the same as the rest. Gorillas are not our ancestors, dolphins are not our cousins, and our pet kittens are not our children. Humanity is set apart from the animal kingdom. We are made in the image of a creatively powerful and awesome God!

In chapter 2 of Genesis, Moses was even more specific about the creation of man. If Genesis 1 is a broad overview of the six days of creation, then Genesis 2 is a commentary on the details of day six, specifically the creation and purpose of humankind.

One of the greatest verses in the entire Bible, one that deals with God's relationship with humanity, is also one of the most glossed over: "The LORD God formed the man of dust from the ground and breathed into his nostrils the breath of life, and the man became a living creature" (Genesis 2:7). Astonishing beauty can be found when you take the time to unpack this verse.

First, God's name changes in this verse. Throughout chapter 1, Moses used the name Elohim for God. However, in this verse he called Him Jehovah Elohim. This subtle but immense detail proclaims the love God has toward His creation, humanity. Elohim, the almighty creator, is also Jehovah Elohim, the friend and counselor of the creature He has created with such care. This all-powerful creator also is a relational God!

Second, throughout Genesis 1, God spoke everything into existence from nothing. He spoke, and it was. However, here it says that He created man *out of the ground*. Instead of making something out of nothing, He chose to make the man out of something He had already made—the dust of the ground—as if to say to the rest of creation that mankind will be better and more beautiful than everything else already created.

Third, think about this little nugget: instead of speaking humanity into existence, God formed them—the man out of the ground, and the woman out of the man's rib. This means that God reached His hands into the dirt and then into the side of the man to begin molding him like a potter at the wheel. It should be incredibly humbling to know that mankind is the only creation in the world for which God got His hands dirty and bloody. Then, on top of it all, He breathed into man "the breath of life." Once again, we should be in awe about the fact that humankind is the only creation of God to share His holy breath. This breath that He shared with us means soul and spirit. He breathed and filled us with a soul and spirit.

God is Spirit, and He created mankind to be spiritual beings. Again, this sets us completely apart from the rest of creation. I know, I know, we may think our pets Fluffy and Sprinkles have souls and spirits. You've most likely heard someone declare, "My puppy and I have such a spiritual connection!" Well, as nice as that sounds, it probably has more to do with Kibbles 'n Bits than spirituality. You feed him. I'm not saying you don't have a connection, but it's definitely not spiritual.

Jehovah Elohim breathed a soul and spirit into humanity so that we would be one with Him. By nature, we are more than bones, flesh, and five senses. We are spiritual beings inside earthly suits made of dirt. In fact, this is why racism shows absolute ignorance and has no place in the kingdom of God. At the end of the day, we're all dirt. Some of us are tall dirt, some are short dirt, some are thin dirt, some are wide dirt, some are white dirt, some are black dirt, some are brown dirt, and some are yellow dirt— but at the end of the day, we're all dirt. What makes all of us valuable and unique is that we all are made in the image of God and have souls and spirits given to us by an all-powerful, relational creator. Ultimately, how we treat others is how we're treating God.

When God created the man and the woman, He created them perfectly. They were fully alive—both physically and spiritually. They were in perfect unity and harmony with their relational God. They were ultimately good. God saw everything He had made and declared it to be "very good" (1:31). Their minds were very good, their intentions were very good, their actions were very good, and their hearts were very good.

So what happened?

In short, the man and woman were placed in the Garden of Eden and given a command by their creator to partake in everything the garden had to offer except from the tree of the knowledge of good and evil. It was an opportunity for humanity to worship their creator by obeying Him, trusting His words, and relying on Him to educate them on what was good and evil instead of experiencing it for themselves. He said, "Adam and Eve, this is all yours—every tree, animal, and fruit. Enjoy it all, but most importantly, enjoy Me as your creator. Trust My command not to eat of one tree, because it will kill you. It will kill your spirit, your soul, and your heart. Disobey what I am telling you, and it will immediately kill you spiritually and will slowly kill you physically. It will literally change everything."

Unfortunately, mankind was not alone in the garden. Satan, taking on the form of a serpent, had slithered his way in. He approached Eve and directly targeted her heart. This story is so much bigger than a woman eating an apple. In fact, we don't even know if it was an apple. The Bible says it was a fruit. It may have been a tangerine, for all we know. However, the fruit is not the point. What happened to the heart of humanity that dreadful day is what's important.

Satan decided to attack Eve the same way he attacks us today. First, he attempted to sow doubt toward the Word of God in the heart of Eve by asking, "Did God actually say . . ." (3:1). Then he called God a liar: "You will not surely die" (verse 4). If he could get Eve to doubt the Word of God and destroy her trust in Him, then attacking her heart would be a piece of cake.

Satan's next statement to the woman was truly the greatest temptation toward the heart of Eve. Once again, it had nothing to do with fruit but had everything to do with trusting God. "God knows that when you eat of it your eyes will be opened, and you will be like God" (verse 5). There it is! That was the temptation that caused all hell to break loose. Mankind no longer needed to trust the Creator, because they could be their own gods! They could now make their own decisions. They could do whatever they wanted because they would determine and define what is good and evil.

Isn't it ironic that the very ideas the serpent used to tempt humankind are the same clichés our culture values so highly as natural rights? "Eve, you don't need God. Be your own God. Believe in yourself. It's your life; do with it what you want. To each their own. Eve, you just need to follow your heart!" She eventually fell to the temptation to be her own god, and her husband followed suit.

Everything immediately changed. Adam changed. Eve changed. Mankind's relationship with its creator changed, and every person born after them would be the same—born dead. We would be spiritually stillborn.

The image of God remains on mankind, but now it's shattered and in desperate need of repair. Humanity went from being declared "very good" to being declared very dead. The spirit inside man and woman, once alive to God and dead to sin, is now alive to sin and dead to God. Humanity in its natural state is spiritually dead. There is nothing we can spiritually do to please a God who is Spirit. The power of sin now reigns in mortal man, making sin the most natural thing for us to do. This affects our minds, our bodies, and our hearts.

This is why our hearts, in their natural state, now pump with deceit, sickness, and foolishness. The heart cannot be trusted. It is not a good leader. We cannot follow it. It is not a loving shepherd leading us to greener pastures. It is a lost and confused sheep that desperately needs rescuing.

Because of this, Jesus had to give us new hearts at salvation. No, our hearts will not save us. We need to be saved from our hearts. Even the prophets of old knew how desperately we needed a major heart change and that the Son of God would fulfill these promises:

> I will give you a new heart, and a new spirit I will put within you. And I will remove the heart of stone from your flesh and give you a heart of flesh. (Ezekiel 36:26)

> I will give them a heart to know that I am the LORD, and they shall be my people and I will be their God, for they shall return to me with their whole heart. (Jeremiah 24:7)

You might even say that Jesus was the first one to perform a heart transplant. Therefore, we should follow the Great Heart Surgeon.

Don't Follow Your Heart . . . Follow Jesus

Jesus did what only God could do. Spiritual death, a shattered image of God, and a broken relationship with the Creator are God-sized problems that only a God-sized man could fix. Jesus, fully man and fully God, lived the life we could not live—the perfect, sin-free life. He died the death we could not die—the perfect sacrifice and substitute for sin. He restored the life we did not have. His victory through the Resurrection provides the way for God's crowning jewel of creation to turn back to Him once again. When the image bearers of God turn to Him for restoration, He gives them His Spirit. When the Spirit of God makes His home inside humanity, everything changes. The shattered image of God is made new. People can be declared good once again. The spirit inside humanity that was alive to sin and dead to God is now alive to God and dead to sin. When the Holy Spirit of God connects with the dead spirits inside people, the Spirit awakens the souls of the people to eternal life. They who once were very dead are now very much alive, never to die again. The pure power of the gospel is not about making good people better; it is about making dead people alive!

We actually become new creations that are once again connected relationally to our creator. This affects our minds, our bodies, and our hearts. Jesus, the shepherd, did what only God could do. He is a trusted guide who will never lead you astray. He is a reliable shepherd who desires to protect His sheep. He is the epitome of everything that is good. This would be a great new and trustworthy one-liner that would provide us with the truth that sets us free: "Don't follow your heart. Follow Jesus." Follow His Word and His Holy Spirit that have been given to us as believers.

Now, someone may ask a very reasonable question: "If Jesus gives us a new heart, then why can't we follow that heart?" The reason we still should not follow our hearts—feelings, emotions, and desires—is because they are still affected by sin. The residue of the fall of humankind still resides in our mortal bodies. It is what is known as the flesh. Our Christian walk can be seen in three major shifts concerning sin. Before Jesus saved us, we were slaves to sin. We couldn't help but sin. As followers of

Jesus, we are now at war with sin. The Spirit of God inside us is waging war against sin. That is why you see the apostle Paul, the spiritual giant who wrote two-thirds of the New Testament, writing things along the lines of "I am the chief of sinners. The things that I hate to do are what I do, and the things that I love to do are not what I do" (see Romans 7; 1 Timothy 1). It's also why many of us can identify so deeply with the lyrics of the hymn "Come, Thou Fount of Every Blessing" that was penned in the 1700s:

> Prone to wander, Lord, I feel it,
> Prone to leave the God I love;
> Here's my heart, O take and seal it;
> Seal it for thy courts above.

Yes, we feel it. We all feel the daily battle of wrestling with our wandering hearts that are prone to leave the God we so desperately love. The war still rages on! But, glory be to God, one day the war will be over. This is the third shift. We were once slaves to sin, are now at war with sin, and one day will truly be freed from all sin. When we stand in the physical presence of our creator, victory will be ours. Sin will be gone, and we will know only righteousness. But we're not there yet.

So, for now, don't follow your heart. Follow Jesus. Don't believe in your heart but instead, diligently direct your heart to believe in God. Notice that Jesus did not say to His disciples, "Hey, guys, let not your hearts be troubled; instead, you just need to try a lot harder to believe in your hearts. Follow them." No, not even a little bit. Rather, He said, "Let not your hearts be troubled. Believe in God; believe also in me" (John 14:1).

To help you make decisions when asking those all-important questions (What career should I choose? Which school should I attend? With whom should I be in a relationship?), God has given you the greatest communicator of all time, Himself! Jesus has given you His Spirit. The Spirit (our helper), who now dwells inside you, speaks to you through His Word, the Bible. He leads you. He answers your questions and shows you the truth of the Bible. You can trust in the Lord with all your heart and not lean on your own understanding because your shepherd will make your paths straight. Your feelings won't be your guide; Jesus will. He is your never-failing GPS. Our hearts were never designed to be gods in whom we believe. No, they were designed to believe in God.

Why is the Bible so important? It's important because whatever is said to us has to align with God's Word. We can rest assured that He will never lead us to do anything that is contrary to it. We are not to follow our hearts. The Holy Spirit leads our hearts. We are to follow Jesus as He constantly shapes and molds our hearts through the power of His Spirit and the tool of His Word.

The battle is always remembering truth. When our hearts try to bow up, desperately wanting to be the boss and leader again, we can know that Jesus is stronger than our hearts. Thank God for this great encouragement in the daily war: "Whenever our heart condemns us, God is greater than our heart, and he knows everything" (1 John 3:20).

Send Off

If I could send you off from this chapter with a revised version of Steve Jobs's graduation speech, it would sound something like this:

> Your time on earth is limited, so don't waste it listening to lies. Don't be trapped by the Deceiver—which is the result of avoiding God's Word. Don't let the noise of others' opinions drown out God's still, small voice. And most important, have the courage to follow Jesus. He knows all you can truly become. Remember He loves you. Everything else is secondary.

Questions for Common Lie 5

1. In the past, where did your mind go when you saw or heard the statement "Follow your heart"? How did this chapter change the way you view that statement?

2. According to this chapter, what is the heart? Read Jeremiah 17:9, Mark 7:21, and Romans 1:21. What does the Bible have to say about our hearts?

3. Our world says, "Do what feels right." Do you think this has damaged our culture? Why or why not?

4. According to this chapter, what or whom should you be following? What has God given you to help lead you in life?

5. This is a great opportunity to think about your own story. Write about the moment when you became a Christian (when Jesus gave you a new heart). If that hasn't happened yet, then it's possible that right now is the perfect time for you to confess Jesus as your lord and savior and ask God to give you a new heart by making His home inside you. If this book has helped you begin a relationship with Jesus Christ, I'd love to hear from you. Please email me at contact@shanepruitt.com.

A Truth to Move Forward With

Don't follow your heart. Follow Jesus.

God Doesn't Really Care

The Lie That Broke My Heart

The beautiful Congolese children were running and playing and yelling, *"Mizungu, Mizungu!"* I found out this basically means "white person from America." They were referring to six of us, visitors who'd come a long, long way to see them. The Congolese adults, however, were a different story. I noticed they looked tired, dejected, and hopeless.

One man who appeared to be in his seventies spoke up as though he was speaking for the whole group. He was the elder of the community. He said, "God loves Uganda, but He has forgotten about us." For a minute, I thought I had heard my translator wrong. I asked, "What did he just say in Swahili?" The translator answered, "He said, 'God loves Uganda, but He has forgotten about us.'" "Well, why does he think that? What does he mean?" The translator asked the gentlemen my question, translating my Texan English into perfect Swahili. The man responded, "God loves Uganda, because He sends a lot of missionaries there. But

God has forgotten about the Congo, because He doesn't send us any."

Wow! It absolutely broke my heart to hear this, for several reasons. The Congolese equated God's love with the presence of God's people, the church. It made me sad for the United States. How we take for granted the presence of the church and the Christian leaders God has blessed America with. Oh, how other countries yearn for what we have. Not our materialism—they can see right through that trap. They yearn for the spiritual things God has blessed us with. Let that be a challenge and conviction to us all. It also broke my heart because he was right. I have personally been to Uganda four times, with many more trips planned in the future. There are missionaries, ministries, orphanages, and churches all over Uganda. Comparatively, there are very, very few in the Democratic Republic of the Congo (DRC). This was my first trip there, but it definitely won't be my last. This country, one-third the size of the United States and home to seventy-eight million people, is in desperate need of hearing about the omnipresent God who has not forgotten about them.

My eyes filled with tears, and my heart pounded in my chest with a thousand beats per second. Immediately, I felt love for these beautiful, beautiful people God has made in His image. With every ounce of sincerity, I said the only thing that could be said in that moment: "God has not forgotten you. He is here. I believe that God is in control, so I would not be with you today in your land unless a holy, on-purpose, and loving God said so. I believe He sent me all this way to tell you this: He loves you, He has not forgotten you, and He is with you."

Over the next five days, I preached more than a dozen times, and I said the very same thing in every village and every church. Without a shadow of a doubt, I believe God sent our team halfway around the globe and too many hours on an airplane watching movies and eating bad food to share with the people of the DRC one message: "God loves the Congo so much that He sent us a very long way to tell you that He loves you, He is with you, He is everywhere, and He has not forgotten you." In no way do I believe God sent us because we were special. He sent us because we were willing to say yes. He also sent us because He deeply loves the people He was sending us to. He had a message for them, and He went to great lengths to share it.

That Congolese elder's words brought to mind the phrase I see and hear from time to time: "God doesn't really care." Sure, it is usually presented as a prod to take responsibility for yourself, to get busy and stop waiting for some variation of the knight in shining armor to ride in and save the day. And while I can understand that, the deeper message this phrase communicates is the absence of a loving God in the universe. Now, the elder wasn't questioning God's existence so much as God's concern. But I fear that for many of us, the distinction between the two gets fuzzy. If God doesn't care, then God may truly be a myth. All this kind of thinking stems from believing that God is like us.

God Does Not Suffer from Amnesia

One of the biggest lies we can believe is that God is exactly like we are. Meaning we often think God struggles with the same failures, limitations, and weaknesses that we do. After all, if I am a certain way, then the One who created me must be the same, right? If I am limited by time and space, then God must be limited by time and space. If I am limited in power, then God must be limited in power. If I break promises, then I bet God breaks His promises too. If I tend to love only those who can love me back, then surely God loves in the same way. If I am limited in knowledge and can easily forget things and people, then God must suffer from forgetfulness as well.

However, this is the fundamental difference between God and us. He is God, and we are not. He is not limited in the ways we are. We may suffer from amnesia (partial or total loss of memory), but He doesn't! You must realize that He is different from you. That is what it means for Him to be holy. Holy means that He is set apart. There is no one, or nothing, like Him. Out of all the things that are, He is completely different from them all. He has characteristics and attributes that only He possesses. Understanding some of these wonderful attributes of God will help you experience freedom from the lie that whispers ever so subtly in your ear, "God doesn't really care."

These attributes are powers only God has. They are God powers. If there were ever a moment when He stopped operating in any one of these powers, He would cease being God because it would mean He was lacking, was in need, and was, sadly, like us. It would mean He was no longer perfect. If He wasn't perfect, then He could easily forget us. Thankfully, this is not like Him at all.

So what are these powers God possesses that prove He needs

nothing at all and is self-sufficient in every way? In particular, there are four characteristics of God that demonstrate He is not like us, is not limited, and will never forget us.

God Is Omnipotent

This is a fancy word that simply means God is all-powerful. God can do everything—possible or impossible. He is not limited. He will do anything He pleases, and He has the power to restrain Himself from doing anything He doesn't want to do. His self-control is absolutely perfect. Nothing is too difficult for Him. God never gets tired. He never forgets. "Jesus looked at them and said, 'With man this is impossible, but with God all things are possible'" (Matthew 19:26). "Have you not known? Have you not heard? The LORD is the everlasting God, the Creator of the ends of the earth. He does not faint or grow weary; his understanding is unsearchable" (Isaiah 40:28).

God Is Omnipresent

He is all-present. God is everywhere, so He doesn't need anyone to take Him anywhere. He never has to pack His suitcase, buy a plane ticket, or ask for a ride in a truck. (Yes, mentioning a truck probably gives it away that I am from Texas.) He is always there. In your home. At your job. There is never a reason to run from Him, hide from Him, or try to escape Him. Wherever you run, He is already there waiting. Pick your favorite hiding spot. He found it first. If you try to escape Him, He is where you were, and He is where you're going. He is running with you as you're going.

He can't forget you because He is right beside you. "Where shall I go from your Spirit? Or where shall I flee from your presence? If I ascend to heaven, you are there! If I make my bed in Sheol, you are there!" (Psalm 139:7–8).

God Is Omnibenevolent

God is all-loving. He loves perfectly and is completely full of love. His love never runs out and never lessens. He can fully and perfectly love 7.5 billion people all at the same time and never lack one ounce of love for someone else. Although He loves perfectly, He doesn't need a relationship with us for Him to be fulfilled. He has a perfectly fulfilled relationship within Himself as the triune God. He is the complete package when it comes to unity. He is the personification of a healthy relationship all within Himself— God the Father, God the Son, and God the Holy Spirit. However, He still loves us perfectly. He doesn't need us for relationship fulfillment, but we desperately need Him because we'll never be fulfilled without Him. God extends His love to us through His Son, Jesus Christ, and the pleasure is truly ours. God meets our needs for love perfectly. "Anyone who does not love does not know God, because God is love" (1 John 4:8).

God Is Omniscient

This is a wonderfully hopeful truth about God that can soothe our depressed hearts. It means that He is all-knowing. There is nothing that anyone can teach Him. He never has to learn anything. There is never a moment when He has to guess, has to be told something, or has to be reminded. Did you catch that? He doesn't have to be reminded, because He never forgets. One more time: He *never* forgets. He remembers everything. He knows where you've been, where you are, and where you're going. Your feelings and emotions may cause you to believe that He has forgotten you, that He has amnesia. However, be reminded of this attribute and never forget that He never forgets. He is greater than your feelings. He knows everything, and that includes you. "Whenever our heart condemns us, God is greater than our heart, and he knows everything" (1 John 3:20).

These attributes of God prove that He doesn't need anything. He doesn't need us to send Him a text message with a map to find us, and He doesn't need us to show Him how to use Google to remember our names. In fact, He doesn't need us at all. However, just because He doesn't need us does not mean He doesn't want us. Every single one of us carries a bit of a savior complex in us. We all love the idea that someone else needs us. Often we long for the moments when the "bat signal" goes up and we can swoop in with our capes to save the day. There are even times when I believe I'm so awesome that the Creator of the universe needs my help to accomplish His will! I like the idea that God somehow needs me.

However, the truth is that even though God doesn't need anything in all the world, He still *wants* me. The cross of Jesus is proof positive that He wants me. He paid the highest price for me. He gave His absolute best to purchase me. Not because I'm awesome or worthy of His redemption but because He lavished me with His amazing grace. He remembered me. He remembers you. He remembers our desperate need for Him.

You may feel that you have no value or that you're some kind of cosmic accident. There are far too many stories in which people have felt useless or unwanted. For example, after I spoke at a large student conference, a seventeen-year-old boy shared with me that his mom told him she had considered aborting him and she wished she would have gone through with it. Or consider the thirteen-year-old girl who told me about the time her father described her as "nothing more than an accident in the back seat of a car." It is a perfectly human reaction to hear these kinds of things and feel useless, purposeless, and unwanted. Even forgotten by God.

However, Scripture paints a different picture: "When the fullness of time had come, God sent forth his Son, born of woman, born under the law, to redeem those who were under the law, so that we might receive adoption as sons. And because you are sons, God has sent the Spirit of his Son into our hearts, crying, 'Abba! Father!' So you are no longer a slave, but a son, and if a son, then an heir through God" (Galatians 4:4–7).

What a beautiful reminder of the truth that God has not forgotten you and that He wants you! He wants you so badly that He was willing to go to any length to redeem you. According to these verses, redemption means that you were once a slave. In fact, you were a slave to sin. There was a ransom—a price tag—on your head that had to be paid in order to set you free. The price tag was death. Jesus paid that price to grant you freedom by dying on the cross, and the Resurrection was your receipt to prove the payment was accepted. You have been set free by the blood of Jesus, and there is nothing more valuable than that. This fact alone places extreme value on your life! God has remembered you.

However, the good news does not stop there. Not only did God pay the ransom to set you free, but He also went one step further by giving you a family to come home to. God could have granted you your freedom and then said, "Good luck out there!" But no! He adopted you and made You His own. He brought you into His family, and your status as an adopted child of God remains forever. He chose you long before you ever had an opportunity to choose Him. He loves you. He wants you. He remembers you.

God's Sending His Son for You Is Proof That He Remembers You

I love everything about the Christmas season—the cheesy Hallmark movies, the family get-togethers, all the over-the-top decorations, and even that fun, competitive game called the white elephant gift exchange. You know this game, right? All the gifts are in the middle, you draw a number, and when it's your turn you either take a gift from the middle or lovingly but decidedly steal the best gift from a particular family member whom you might not even really like very much. There have actually been grudges started and sustained that can be attributed to rounds of this game. I'm only slightly joking.

However, when it comes to gifts, God gave us the greatest gift of all. You could even say God gave us His very best—Himself! Jesus, the Son of God, came to us, gave Himself up for us, and gave us the opportunity to experience eternal life.

Jesus truly was Immanuel, *God with us.* This is what is commonly called the incarnation of Christ, which means that the Son of God came to earth and became fully man (He also remained fully God) to live with mankind. The incarnation of Christ is one of the most beautiful teachings of Scripture. When you realize the incredible truths behind the reality that God came and dwelt among us, it can't help but influence the way you live. Unfortunately, it's a truth we're often reminded of only during the Christmas season. We need to be reminded of this beautiful promise every single day of our lives. He is with you. "Behold, I am with you always, to the end of the age" (Matthew 28:20). You are never alone. You are not forgotten. You are remembered. As a child of God, you don't just celebrate the arrival of the Son of God one day a year on December 25. You have the ability now to live and walk in this freedom. Celebrate it every moment of every day of the year.

The incarnation of Christ is proof that He always remembers you. He remembers you because He is with you. Always. This truth can be trusted. He can be trusted. Let me explain the reasoning behind this truth.

God Has Proven Himself

Often in frustration or doubt, people will exclaim, "God, if You're real, then prove it! Show Yourself. If You really care about us and remember us, then come down here and communicate to us." Interestingly, that is *exactly* what He did in Jesus. God proved Himself. He cares about you. The apostle Paul told the church in Colossae that Jesus is "the image of the invisible God" (Colossians 1:15). He made God visible. Want to know what God is like? Look to Jesus! Want to see the face of God? Look into the face of Jesus. Want to know that God remembers you? Look to the love of His Son, Jesus.

God Always Keeps His Promises

We've all been hurt by broken promises. They may have been broken vows, broken covenants, or broken commitments. They hurt, they sting, and they leave a wake of deep wounds. But if we're honest with ourselves, as imperfect people, we've also hurt others by breaking our promises to them. However, God always keeps His promises. If He says it, He will do it. He can be fully trusted. "For all the promises of God find their Yes in him. That is why it is through him that we utter our Amen to God for his glory" (2 Corinthians 1:20). The Old Testament is one big promise that a savior, deliverer, and rescuer was coming. There are over three hundred prophecies (promises) in the Old Testament about the coming Messiah, and Jesus fulfilled every single one of them. God is the ultimate promise keeper! He told us that He remembered us, He loves us, and He was coming for us. God has not forgotten you. He kept His promise to you. "It is he who remembered us in our low estate, for his steadfast love endures forever" (Psalm 136:23).

God Has Come and Is Coming Again

God kept His promise of the first coming of Jesus. He completely proved Himself to be trustworthy. He did not forget. He remembered. Therefore, you can also fully trust the promises made by God that Christ is coming again. Just like the Old Testament saints were eagerly waiting for the first coming, we as New Testament saints are eagerly awaiting His second coming. In fact, there are more prophecies in the Scriptures about Jesus's second coming than there are about His first. What great hope this provides. He remembers you. He knows your struggles, your suffering, and your sadness. He knows when you feel forgotten. Yet He still loves you and remembers you. His promise to you is that your suffering will have an expiration date. The way things are now is not the way they will always be. He is coming back because He remembers you. However, His second coming will look drastically different from His first:

- The first time Jesus came to earth, He came as a baby. When He comes back, He will come as a full-grown king.
- The first time Jesus came to earth, He came lying in a manger. When He comes back, He will come riding a white horse.
- The first time Jesus came to earth, He came in weakness and meekness. When He comes back, He will come in power and glory.
- The first time Jesus came to earth, He came to

pay for the sins of the world. When He comes
back, He will do away with all sin.

- The first time Jesus came to earth, He came as a
  suffering servant. When He comes back, He will
  come as a conquering master.
- The first time Jesus came to earth, He came as a
  sacrificial lamb. When He comes back, He will
  come as a roaring lion.
- The first time Jesus came to earth, He suffered
  momentarily on the cross. When He comes back,
  He will make sure that Satan will suffer for all
  eternity in hell.
- The first time Jesus came to earth, very few people in
  a town called Bethlehem knew about it. When He
  comes back, everyone on earth will know who He is.
- The first time Jesus came to earth, only a few wise
  men bowed down before Him. When He comes
  back, every knee will bow down before Him.

There will, however, be a few similarities:

- The first time Jesus came to earth, He came because
  He loves you. When He comes back, He will come
  because He loves you.
- The first time Jesus came to earth, He came because
  He remembered you. When He comes back, He will
  come because He remembers you.

Yes, contrary to popular belief, Someone has come and is
coming again. He cares. And His name is Jesus.

The Presence of God Brings a Presence of Peace

A segment of my Congolese friends feel as though they have been forgotten by God. They are stricken with poverty in a way that most Americans could never understand. These precious people do not choose their favorite brand of bottled water. Instead, they walk for miles every day in search of clean water. They do not stress over getting their yards mowed before the homeowners' association tickets them, because they live in mud huts with red dirt floors and yards. They don't have to take out the trash at night, because they don't have anything to throw away. They're not hoping for the newest video game system. They're hoping for food, basic medicine, and protection from militia groups.

If I'm honest with myself—if you're honest with yourself—we have to understand why they would feel forgotten by God. Put in the same circumstances, I might feel the same way. Especially if I had the perception that God was sending His people and His resources to my neighbors. I may think, *God, thank You for blessing them, but You drove right by me to go to them. You give them a loaf of bread, and I can't even have a crumb. You're sending thousands of Your people there and can't send one here?* It's easy to be entrapped by the perception of God forgetting you when you're constantly in the direst of situations. Who can blame someone for that? Surely we're not so naive to believe that we could never fall into the same trap. It's easy to claim that God is with you and remembers you when everything is going your way, when all your needs are met, and when everything makes sense. But what about when nothing is going your way, when your needs are not met, and when nothing makes sense? Can you still stand on the promise that God is with you then?

While we met many people in the Democratic Republic of the Congo who felt hopeless, joyless, and forgotten, there were other folks too. Different folks with different demeanors and different words. They had joy. They had peace. They had perspective of God's love for them. Don't get me wrong. These people still had the same circumstances and struggles. They had to search for water and food. They struggled with the same sicknesses. They lived in the same huts. They were poor in the world's eyes, yet they were the richest people I had ever met. They were rich in love. They were rich in joy. They were rich in peace.

Why were they so different from their neighbors who lived a few kilometers down the same road? What did they have that the others didn't? It wasn't money. It wasn't better access to clean water and good food. It wasn't a nicer hut. It wasn't that more missionaries were visiting them, while ignoring their neighbors. So what was it? Maybe a better question is, *Who* was it?

Simply, they had the Holy Spirit of God living inside them. They knew their God was with them, in them, and looking after them. They knew they were not forgotten, even in their time of distress. "In my distress I called to the LORD, and he answered me" (Psalm 120:1).

God doesn't ever promise you an easy road or freedom from suffering. But He does promise to be with you. When you recognize His presence, there will be joy there, love there, and peace there because He is there. "For he himself is our peace" (Ephesians 2:14).

Don't believe the lie. Hold tight to the truth. God has not forgotten you. He remembers you. He is with you. Because you are a Christian, He is inside you. Wherever you are, there He is. And you can have peace knowing He is not going to leave you. "Be strong and courageous. Do not fear or be in dread of them, for it is the LORD your God who goes with you. He will not leave you or forsake you" (Deuteronomy 31:6).

Questions for Common Lie 6

1. Have you ever felt as though God had forgotten you or didn't really care about you? What was going on then?

2. In the section titled "God Does Not Suffer from Amnesia," what four characteristics of God were discussed? Which one of those characteristics resonated with you the most? How can you incorporate that truth into your life?

3. Read Galatians 4:4–7. What words or phrases stand out to you when you read these verses? How does it make you feel to know that God chose to adopt you as His child?

4. What does the incarnation of Christ mean? How does this influence the way you view your daily life? How will it affect you this week?

5. According to this chapter, what are some differences between Jesus's first coming and His second coming? Does this cause you to live with fear or encouragement or a different emotion? What aspect of seeing Jesus face to face are you most excited about?

A Truth to Move Forward With

God has not forgotten you. He remembers
you. He is with you.

Well, _____ Will Never Change

Who's in Your Blank?

One of the greatest lies the devil uses to discourage followers of Jesus is that "_____ will never change." So who's in your blank? Most likely, that person is someone you deeply love and care about. The worry over her keeps you up at night, has resulted in a stomach ulcer or two, and has caused many tears to be shed. Maybe this person is a child, a grandchild, a parent, a sibling, or a close friend. You've lost hope because you believe she will never change.

On the other hand, the person in your blank could be someone who stirs anger inside you. He is dreadful. He enjoys his sin, and at least from the outside looking in, it seems he couldn't care less how it affects other people. Maybe, in moments of frustration, you've described him and his actions as pure evil. This person could be an ex-spouse, a dishonest boss, a cantankerous neighbor, or even a world leader who is causing all kinds of problems for the citizens he is supposed to be serving. To make this even more relevant, groups of people may be affected by demonic influences that thrive off other people's fears, causing them to commit acts of terror, torture, and turmoil. It is easy to look at their actions and say these people are beyond any hope of change.

Whether the person in your blank is someone you love, someone you resent, or someone who stirs both of those emotions, if you have fallen into the belief that she will never change, then it's time for you to be the one who changes. You need to realize you're believing a lie. You've got the emphasis in the wrong place, focusing on an impossible person instead of the God of the impossible. You see, it's not "Who's in your blank?" It's "Whom do you trust?" God is her creator, He still loves her, and He has the power to change her. No one is too far gone. There is no human still alive who is outside the possible reach of God's forgiving and transforming grace. In your eyes, it may appear to be an impossible situation. However, there is hope. The hope is that there is a God who loves to make the impossible possible. "Jesus looked at them and said, 'With man this is impossible, but with God all things are possible'" (Matthew 19:26). "For nothing will be impossible with God" (Luke 1:37).

I follow Beth Moore on Twitter (you should too). She tweeted this on April 16, 2018: "I still believe people can change. I still believe in the transforming power of the gospel & not only to save the lost. I believe in something the world might find truly astonishing: that Jesus can change US, change our minds, remove our blind spots. I still believe in good news." Amen, Beth Moore, amen—with God, we all can change.

With God

One of my favorite stories of life change is my father-in-law's testimony and his journey. When I first met Kasi, her relationship with her father was nearly nonexistent. She would have told you she believed that a healthy relationship with her dad was nearly impossible. Their situation seemed beyond hope, her father seemed beyond the possibility of change, and their relationship seemed beyond repair. She would have said, "Dad will never change." But with God? Well, that's another story.

Growing up, Kasi was always a daddy's girl. She remembers crawling up in her dad's lap and watching their favorite shows together on Friday nights. She absolutely adored him, and her dad loved her too. He loved his family and worked very hard to provide for them, but he also loved something else—alcohol. And lots of it.

When Kasi was a young child, her parents were always very affectionate and loving toward each other. However, in her preteen years, they became very distant. The dynamic of their home changed because of her father's love for alcohol. He also made some other really bad decisions. Decisions that would change everything forever.

One night, after one of those massive mistakes, her mom finally had enough and decided to divorce her dad. Kasi still remembers the day her mom told her and her brother. That memory is burned into her subconscious. It's easy for Kasi to put herself back in that room and recall every dreadful and painful word of that conversation. She was devastated. Her brother was terrified. She believed her life as she knew it was over.

When Kasi was just thirteen years old, her parents divorced. Her mother wanted a fresh start, so she and Kasi moved to a different town, away from everything Kasi had ever known. It was just the two of them now because her older brother was living on the campus of the university he was attending. Her dad quickly spiraled downward, and she hardly ever saw or talked to him. He would call her on birthdays and major holidays, and she would see him every now and then, but their relationship was strained at best. He would randomly show up at Kasi's ball games but would sit in the visitors' bleachers or on the opposite side of the gymnasium.

Kasi would lie in her room at night, wondering how a former daddy's girl was now a forgotten girl. She became incredibly bitter toward him and could not understand why he had chosen other things over his family. And she essentially lost hope that anything could fix their relationship, thinking, *Dad will never change.*

There was a time when Kasi believed that her mom's decision to move them to another town was a horrible idea, but it turned out to be one of the best things that could have ever happened to her. After they moved, they began attending a local church. She had not grown up going to church, so this was something new for her, and she loved every minute of it. It felt like a safe place, a hopeful place, and, most importantly, a loving place.

It was also during this time that Kasi came face to face with her relationship with Jesus. For a while, she had believed that being a Christian just meant you went to church when you had some free time. But when she was fifteen years old, she came to a different realization. Kasi went with members of her church to a student camp for junior high and high school students. It proved to be a truly life-changing week in which God opened her eyes to the fact that just being inside a church building doesn't make you a Christian any more than going to McDonald's makes you a Happy Meal. To become a Christian, you must turn from your sin and put your trust in Jesus as your king and savior. She took a bold step of faith that night by laying her life down and trusting Jesus to take control of it. Kasi has never been the same since that week.

Ironically, sometimes God doesn't change the hearts of the people we care deeply about until He first changes ours. Kasi's love for Jesus caused her heart to be changed, and therefore, her feelings toward her dad and her prayers for him began to change. She started calling him more, and she started praying with desperation that God would intervene in his life. She prayed with faith to a God who makes the impossible possible. She now believed He was a God of possibilities who changed impossible people for His glory every single day. She also prayed that God would give her the strength to forgive her dad. At this point, he hadn't even asked for it and sure didn't deserve it, but she had the conviction that in order for God to bring healing, she had to forgive him. Forgiveness often is a journey and doesn't happen overnight. All acts of forgiveness need at least three components: God, grace, and time. Over time, the bitterness started to melt away. Kasi kept praying and pleading with God to grant her dad salvation and life transformation. She longed for him to personally know Jesus and to enjoy the same freedom she did.

Then came our wedding day in 2004. The glorious day that I married way, way over my head. It was the day when Kasi and I would stand before God and our assembled witnesses to make a covenant to Him and to each other. One of those witnesses at the church that day was Kasi's father. It was the day God started to reveal to her that He was about to do something crazy awesome in her dad's life. Right before her dad was supposed to walk her down the aisle, he came into the room and asked to talk to Kasi. After everyone left the room, he grabbed her hands and said, "Kasi, I need to apologize to you. I haven't been there for you the way I should. I know I have missed out on so much, and I am sorry. I want things to change, and I want us to be close again." She could not fight back the tears as they began rolling down her beautiful face. It was then that she knew the past five years of begging God to rescue her dad were going to pay off. She believed that with God it would happen.

Several months after our wedding day, I went on a mission trip to Israel. While I was gone, Kasi's father asked her to go to the horse races with him. She had never been before, but any opportunity to spend time with her dad sounded great to her. Once they arrived, they sat down in the bleachers and began a pleasant conversation filled with surface-level small talk. Then the conversation began to shift. Her father spoke with nervousness but also with clarity. "Kasi, I need to ask you something. When I am with you, there is just something different about you. I don't know what it is. You have a joy. It's hard to explain, but you are different than most people I know." She couldn't believe it! It was as if all those years of praying, crying, and pleading with God all came down to this very moment. She said, "The only way for me to tell you how I am different is by telling you about my Jesus." So Kasi began telling him about the good news of the gospel.

Once she was done sharing with her dad, he looked at her and said, "Well, now that I know what makes you so different, I want that too." So right there at the horse races, her dad prayed and asked Jesus to come into his life and make him a new person. Kasi still talks about that day with joy on her face and tears in her eyes. She'll never forget it. From that day forward, everything began to change for the better and was never the same again. With God all things are possible.

Today, Kasi's dad is one of the most treasured people in our lives. He calls her often. We eat dinner with him at least once a week. He comes to all his grandchildren's ball games and activities. He doesn't sit on the opposite side of the gym anymore. He sits in the middle of us all and takes his grandchildren to the concession stand to spoil them and buy all the snacks they can handle. He was baptized and is now heavily involved in a local church. He is a changed man. He is a new creation in Christ. "If anyone is in Christ, he is a new creation. The old has passed away; behold, the new has come" (2 Corinthians 5:17).

This is a wonderful story, but maybe your story is different. Maybe you haven't seen God change the person in your life. The tears, the begging, and the worrying are all still very real for you. Maybe the story of Kasi and her dad gives you hope. Or, if you were to be honest, maybe their story brings on more frustration and heartbreak because it seems as if God is changing everyone except the person you've been praying for. You've tried to be hopeful, but it feels as though she'll never change.

We Have a Father Who Runs with Love

The parable of the prodigal son from Luke 15 is one of the most well-known stories from the Bible. There are tons of people who know next to nothing about the Bible but still know something about this narrative. It's also one of the greatest redemption stories ever told. It's a story filled with love, mercy, and grace. This parable is given to us as an illustration of how our heavenly Father views us, accepts us, and forgives us when we repent and come home to Him.

We can also learn from this parable how we should and should not respond when a prodigal returns home. We can all identify with this story. It's easy to see yourself as one of the characters, whether you're the grieving father, the wayward son experiencing the party life, or the elder brother who stayed close to the father while his brother strayed. In fact, in the ebb and flow of life, you may be able to identify with different characters during different stages of your own journey. Maybe you were once the wayward child, but now you're the grieving parent. Perhaps you were once the bitter brother who never left, but now you understand the unconditional love of the father because your child or grandchild has strayed and you'd give anything for him to come home.

As a reminder, let's take a look at this great story once again.

> There was a man who had two sons. And the younger
> of them said to his father, "Father, give me the share of
> property that is coming to me." And he divided his
> property between them. (verses 11–12)

The son was asking for his inheritance that he normally wouldn't receive until his father passed away. Think about it. This action spoke loudly to his father: "Give me my inheritance now. I'm leaving. You'll be dead to me as I go and experience what the world has to offer." Can you identify with this father? Possibly the actions of a loved one who has strayed make you feel as though you're dead to her.

This son left his father, his home, and everything he had ever known to go sow his wild oats and live it up. After all, you only live once, right? However, the world was not kind to him. He went from the party scene to the pig scene. You know you're in bad shape when you begin to covet what the hogs have. He had officially hit rock bottom.

> When he came to himself, he said, "How many of my
> father's hired servants have more than enough bread,
> but I perish here with hunger! I will arise and go to my
> father, and I will say to him, 'Father, I have sinned
> against heaven and before you. I am no longer worthy
> to be called your son. Treat me as one of your hired
> servants.'" And he arose and came to his father. (verses
> 17–20)

Sometimes you pray for your beloved prodigal to hit bottom, because often that fall is the only thing that will wake him up. You pray that he won't stay and wallow on the bottom but that it will be a learning experience, making him want to rise and never go back there again. One of the most grievous tragedies is when someone hits bottom and stays there or, worse yet, doesn't even realize he's at the bottom. Everyone can see it but him. However, in this story, the son realizes how far he has strayed and decides it's time to go home. Most likely, this is the response you've been praying for. Maybe you've been praying for your friend, your child, or your parent to have a life transformation. Oh, what a glorious day it will be when she realizes how much better it is with her heavenly Father than where she currently is.

In verse 17 it says that "he came to himself." This means he had an awakening, an epiphany, that caused him to realize what he must do—return to his home. With the return came repentance and confession. He said, "I have sinned against heaven and before you" (verse 18). Before someone can truly reconcile with you, he must reconcile with God. Only God can change an impossible heart in a way that will lead to the reconciliation that makes a healthy relationship possible.

> While he was still a long way off, his father saw him and
> felt compassion, and ran and embraced him and kissed
> him. And the son said to him, "Father, I have sinned
> against heaven and before you. I am no longer worthy to
> be called your son." But the father said to his servants,
> "Bring quickly the best robe, and put it on him, and put

a ring on his hand, and shoes on his feet. And bring the
fattened calf and kill it, and let us eat and celebrate. For
this my son was dead, and is alive again; he was lost, and
is found." And they began to celebrate. (verses 20–24)

There is so much we can learn from the father in this great
story. To understand grace, you need to understand the father,
and to understand the father, you need to understand the culture
at the time this story was told. In the first century, a Middle Eastern man never ran. And I mean never. These men wore tunics that
reached nearly to their sandals. So if a man were to run, he would
have to pick up the bottom of his tunic so that he wouldn't trip
and fall. In doing this, he would show his bare legs. In that culture, it would have been humiliating and shameful for a man to
show his bare legs.

However, this father broke all those cultural molds to run and
meet his son. He was a father who ran with love! You can see incredible joy here. You can see incredible compassion here. You can
see incredible grace and forgiveness here. The father ran, bringing
shame on himself, to make the son feel welcomed home. Don't
forget that by asking for his inheritance, the son had basically told
his father that he was dead to him. Yet here is the father sacrificing
so much to forgive his son and welcome him back. He ran to him,
embraced him, put his best robe on him, put a ring on him, and
killed a calf for a feast. If you'll notice, it cost the son nothing,
while all the cost fell upon the father. Isn't that exactly how the
gospel is? We reject the Father with a sinful lifestyle. We squander
everything God gives us in pursuit of the false pleasures the world

promises us. But when we turn toward the Father, He runs to embrace us, welcomes us home, and lavishes us with His good gifts. And to do this, it cost Him everything, primarily the sacrifice of His Son on the cross. There is nothing we bring back home with us besides heartache, embarrassment, and shame. Nevertheless, He is overwhelmed with joy when we come home, and He celebrates our homecoming. He loves prodigals, and His love causes our heartache, embarrassment, and shame to melt away. "Just so, I tell you, there is joy before the angels of God over one sinner who repents" (verse 10).

Preparing for Prodigals to Come Home

As the prodigal returns, there is another kind of response that is very different from the father's.

> Now his older son was in the field, and as he came and drew near to the house, he heard music and dancing. And he called one of the servants and asked what these things meant. And he said to him, "Your brother has come, and your father has killed the fattened calf, because he has received him back safe and sound." But he was angry and refused to go in. His father came out and entreated him, but he answered his father, "Look, these many years I have served you, and I never disobeyed your command, yet you never gave me a young goat, that I might celebrate with my friends. But when this son of yours came, who has devoured your property with prostitutes, you killed the

fattened calf for him!" And he said to him, "Son, you are
always with me, and all that is mine is yours. It was fitting
to celebrate and be glad, for this your brother was dead,
and is alive; he was lost, and is found." (verses 25–32)

Sometimes it's easy to understand and identify with the
prodigal son or the grieving father. But what about this older
brother? Often we don't as quickly identify with him, but I fear
that many of us are more like him than we'd care to admit.

Honestly evaluate your thoughts and feelings. Are you ready
for that prodigal in your life to return? Would you show her the
same love, compassion, and forgiveness that the father does? If
God forgave her unconditionally, would you place conditions on
her to gain your forgiveness? Would you be able to truly rejoice at
her return and go a step above by richly blessing her at the expense
of yourself? I don't know about you, but thinking through these
questions is causing me to feel a lot more like the older brother.
His response is starting to make a lot more sense, isn't it? Of course
he had the right to be angry and confused by his father's response.
After all, he was the one who stayed at home, did all the chores,
and had to cover all the work in the fields that his younger brother
left behind. He saw firsthand his father's heartbreak and witnessed
the tears night after night as his father stared down the road, wondering if his son was ever coming home. Can't you just see this
brother's bitterness grow each night when he came into the house
tired, sweaty, and sore from doing the work of two in the fields
from sunup till sundown?

Ironically, this elder brother was just as prodigal as his younger brother. Wait, what? How? He stayed. He worked. He didn't ask for his inheritance and then go squander it all away. How was he also a prodigal? He was a prodigal because he strayed relationally and spiritually. He said, "Look, these many years I have served you" (verse 29). Notice he didn't say, "All these years I have loved you. I know you've been waiting for your son to come home, and I am so excited because I love you. I've always respected you, adored you, and trusted your responses." It's almost as though he was saying, "I've served you. Now you owe me." The rest of the sentence also reveals his prodigal heart: "yet you never gave me a young goat" (verse 29). How confusing that must have been for the father. What? He is mad about a goat? It would make a little more sense if he was mad that he didn't get a boat. But no! He wanted a goat. However, I think we can all agree that the goat was just an outlet for a deeper issue—his own waywardness. This was how he viewed his relationship with his father. He worked for his father and never physically left, but he felt he had a right to dictate how his father should respond to his younger brother. In fact, he even felt justified in demanding that his father give him his rightful goat. Ironically, isn't that how the younger son treated the father at first as well? Demanding things from him? Sadly, this elder brother was not prepared for his prodigal brother to return, because he was a prodigal himself. Notice he refused to call him his brother: "But when this son of yours . . ." (verse 30). His judgment was so harsh and hateful that he wouldn't even acknowledge that the prodigal was related to him.

Yet the hardest pill to swallow for you and me is that we understand him. Especially if you grew up in the church and feel as if you've never strayed. It makes it easy to cast judgment on those who have. Somehow you get to the place where you think you've earned the Father's love and attention. Once you think you've earned it, you lose sight of grace and begin to look down on those who, in your opinion, have not earned it the same way you have.

At the end of the day, you can't control what the person you love so much is going to do. You can't make him come home. You can't open his eyes for him. You can't make him realize he is in the pigpen. Only God can open his eyes and change his heart. Then, even after that, he has to decide whether he is going to return. You can't control it. You can't make him. You can't change him. And even if you could, it still wouldn't be the life transformation that comes only from the Father, who makes the impossible possible. A person can't change simply to make you happy. Real change has to come from the Father for His glory.

Although you can't control the person you love, you're still not helpless in the situation. You can practice self-control by being prepared for his return if he does ever decide to come home. You don't have to sit idly by. Do the work that flows from the love of your great Father to make sure you're prepared to respond the same way He does. Basically, be ready to pick up your tunic and run!

What are some things you can do to make sure you're prepared for your prodigal to come home? How can you be ready to run to him and wrap your arms around him? Well, to begin with, if you find yourself with thoughts similar to the older brother's, then you are not prepared for your prodigal to return. First, you need to repent of your own prodigal heart and return to your heavenly Father yourself. You need to be reminded of the Father's grace in your own life. Be reminded of the blessings He has showered upon you at the cost of His Son. Be reminded of the unconditional love He has shown you. Have you strayed from that love you felt when you first came home? Now is the time to return to it. "I have this against you, that you have abandoned the love you had at first" (Revelation 2:4).

Second, a prepared person is a praying person. We should never talk to people about God until we talk to God about people. Can you say you are truly praying for the prodigal? There is a difference between begging God to rescue someone from the pigpen and complaining to Him about the person in the pigpen. Can you honestly say your heart is burdened for that prodigal because she has sinned against God, or are you more bothered that she has hurt your feelings? Pray that she will be made right with God first. Often when people get right with God, they then get right with those they have hurt so badly. Are you praying to God with faith that He can do the impossible? Do you really believe He can change this person? Don't pray with doubt. Pray with confidence, knowing that your Father wants to see her rise from the pigpen and come home even more than you do. It's hard to imagine, isn't it? That God loves this person even more than you do? I promise you, it's true. Pray as though it is true. I wish I could fully explain to you the power of prayer, but I can't. Mainly because my little brain can't completely understand how prayer works. However, there is one thing I know for sure. Praying will move the heart of God in a way that silence won't. Very simply, prayer has power when it is directed toward an all-powerful God who works at making the impossible possible. "This is the confidence that we have toward him, that if we ask anything according to his will he hears us" (1 John 5:14).

Last, in the meantime, don't intentionally burn any bridges. Throughout the years that I've served in ministry, I've heard some other pastors and Christian leaders give really bad advice. Believe me, I've given my own fair share of bad advice as well. Telling people they should treat their prodigal loved ones with tough love, shut them out, close the door on them, or cut them off from the family is often the worst thing you can do. Now, please don't hear me wrong. In no way am I saying you should be a doormat for your prodigal, continue to enable his dangerous behavior, or even expose your other loved ones to him if he is not healthy to be around. What I am saying is this: you don't see Jesus treating wayward and struggling sinners with aggression and tough love. Have you ever noticed that He was most patient, loving, and compassionate toward sinners and outcasts and most aggressive, impatient, and harsh toward the religious leaders of the day who operated in legalism rather than grace? Basically, you see Jesus hanging out with sinners and avoiding those who were self-righteous.

> As he reclined at table in his house, many tax collectors
> and sinners were reclining with Jesus and his disciples, for
> there were many who followed him. And the scribes of the
> Pharisees, when they saw that he was eating with sinners
> and tax collectors, said to his disciples, "Why does he eat

with tax collectors and sinners?" And when Jesus heard it, he said to them, "Those who are well have no need of a physician, but those who are sick. I came not to call the righteous, but sinners." (Mark 2:15–17)

Who knows, God may not bring your prodigal home because you're not emotionally or spiritually ready for him to come back. I wonder how many times the Lord desires the prodigal to return, and even the prodigal desires to come home, yet you have burned the bridge for him to return on. The fire from your fierce bitterness, anger, and tough love can burn down the very bridge on the path of reconciliation, leaving him no way to come back even if he wanted to. Remember, it is the Lord's kindness that leads to repentance, not your wrath (see Romans 2:4).

The Power of God on a Ladder

I want to encourage you not to give up on the person in your blank, whoever that person is for you. As long as she's breathing and as long as God is still God, there is a way. There is hope. Nothing is impossible with Him.

There was a time when Kasi would have said, "My dad will never change." However, God has changed not only her dad but also her whole family for the better. Her mom decided to wait until her kids were all grown and married before she would date again. She later met a wonderful man who loves God, and they got married not long after they started seeing each other. They've now been married for over ten years. Kasi's dad is still single but is currently dating a great woman.

And it wasn't too long ago that we got to witness firsthand the power of God in a subtle but powerful way—on a ladder. We were all at a church building to do some cleaning and remodeling. As Kasi and I were walking through groups of hardworking people, while giving our encouragements and greetings (after all, we pastors and Christian leaders are usually better at encouraging others who are doing manual labor than we are at doing it ourselves), we walked up to a work project that took our breath away.

Two men on a ladder were working together to hang a new light fixture. They were laughing and talking as though they'd been great friends since high school. Who were those two men? Kasi's dad on the left side of the ladder and her stepdad on the right. They never noticed us standing there gawking. There were plenty of men to do the work, plenty of projects to be done, and plenty of ladders to use. Yet these two men were doing this particular project on the same ladder.

After a few long seconds, my wife looked at me and said, "Look at them. In what world would you ever see a man standing on a ladder helping another man who married his ex-wife?"

The following statement just kind of slid out of my mouth: "Never in a million years did I think I'd see that. That definitely doesn't make sense in our society today. What in the world is going on?"

Kasi simply replied, "What is going on is the power of a God who can change people."

The only thing I knew to say at that point was, "Yep. And on a ladder, of all places."

Then we both walked away holding hands, confident yet thankful smiles on our faces.

Questions for Common Lie 7

1. So who is in your blank? If you're honest, has there been a time when you believed God couldn't change him? How did this chapter help you see this person differently?

2. What part of Kasi's story with her dad did you connect with the most? Does this give you hope for the future? Why or why not?

3. Read Luke 15:11–32, the story of the prodigal son. Whom do you connect with most in the story—the father, the son who strayed, or the son who stayed? Why?

4. What are some ways you can stay prepared for the person in your blank to be changed, for that prodigal to come home?

5. Take this time to do some soul searching. Do you really want this person to change? Would she be welcomed back in your life if she did? Are you prepared for her to return? How often do you pray for her? Stop right now and pray for the person in your blank by name.

A Truth to Move Forward With

Nothing is impossible for God. He has the power to change people so they will start living the life He desires for them.

I Don't Think God Likes Me

Loves and Likes and Fondness

It was the middle of July, and I was speaking at a student summer camp in West Texas. This particular Thursday night was just like every other West Texas night during this time of year—a breezy 182 degrees. Okay, I may be exaggerating, but only by a little bit.

There we were in a metal building that had a seating capacity of five hundred, with about seven hundred sweaty teenagers crammed in like sardines in a can. Because it was toward the end of the week, there was a certain musk in the air: the aroma of hundreds of fifteen-year-olds who naively equated swimming in a pool all week with taking a shower. There is nothing like a worship center filled with a dense fog of filth, adolescent stench, and enough Axe body spray to choke a moose.

That night, I had preached on a familiar passage from John chapter 3. Of course, I focused on verse 16: "For God so loved the world, that he gave his only Son, that whoever believes in him should not perish but have eternal life." As sweat dripped from the tip of my nose onto the highlighted passages of my Bible, I pled with the students to experience, enjoy, and be encouraged by the truth that God loves them and sent His very best for them—His only Son. I told them, "He loves you with a perfect love, so don't ever get over it. Be overwhelmed by it, rest in it, and love others out of the overflow of it. The three most powerful words in the English language are 'God loves you.'"

As I wrapped up this message, the band came back up to sing a popular worship song at the time, "How He Loves." While the lyrics were blaring in the background, "Oh, how He loves. Yeah, He loves us, oh, how He loves us," students began responding by praying at the stage and with their pastors and leaders. Tears were flowing from the overwhelming beauty of this God who loves His people.

While soaking up the wonder of this moment, I noticed out of the corner of my eye a young man who was standing about ten feet from me, looking as though he wanted to speak with me but didn't know how to approach. I walked over to him, and he indicated he wanted to talk. We stepped outside the worship center so that we could hear each other. I learned that his name was Jeff. He was eighteen years old and had just graduated from high school. He was headed to junior college after the summer to play basketball.

"So, Jeff. What's going on, man?"

"Well, Shane, I appreciate what you had to say about how God loves me. However, it's hard for me to swallow that because

I don't even think God likes me. In fact, I am certain that God really doesn't like me very much at all!"

"Wait. What? You don't think God likes you? You think He is mad at you? Did He schedule to fight you at the playground after school or something?" (Yes, unfortunately I often operate with the spiritual gift of sarcasm.)

"Ha. Nah, man. Nothing like that. I just don't think God likes me. I work really hard to keep His rules, but I still struggle with sin. I try really hard to overcome my problems, and I can't. I pray and go to church. For the most part I am a really good person. However, I am so certain that He doesn't like me that I am starting to not like Him very much either."

I appreciated Jeff's honesty. And I understood what he was saying, how it's hard to believe that anyone, much less God, could love you if he really didn't like you. That exchange brought to mind the story Brennan Manning used to tell about his friend Edward Farrell, a priest from Detroit:

[Ed] went on a two-week summer vacation to Ireland to visit relatives. His one living uncle was about to celebrate his eightieth birthday. On the great day, Ed and his uncle got up early. It was before dawn. They took a walk along the shores of Lake Killarney and stopped to watch the sunrise. They stood side by side for a full twenty minutes and then resumed walking. Ed glanced at his uncle and saw that his face had broken into a broad smile. Ed said, "Uncle Seamus, you look very happy."

"I am." Ed asked, "How come?" And his uncle replied, "The Father of Jesus is very fond of me."*

What about you? Do you honestly believe God likes you—not loves you, because theologically He must—but truly likes you? God loves by necessity of His nature; without the eternal, interior generation of love, He would cease to be God. But if you could answer, "The Father is very fond of me," there would come a relaxedness, a serenity, and a compassionate attitude toward yourself that reflects God's own tenderness. In Isaiah 49:15, God says, "Can a woman forget her nursing child, that she should have no compassion on the son of her womb? Even these may forget, yet I will not forget you."

The Two Ditches of Self-Righteousness

Ed's uncle had lived a long time and no doubt had wrestled with much to get to a place of peace where he could say, "The Father of Jesus is very fond of me." But Jeff was young—very young—and the road he would take following our conversation was very important, for here's the plain and simple truth: working really hard to get God to like you is a fruit of self-righteousness. And what is that? It's the effort to become righteous before God by your own efforts. Self-righteousness is always defined by self. You decide what is right and wrong. You vainly attempt to define what is good enough to please God. Or, more accurately, you determine

---

* Brennan Manning, *The Relentless Tenderness of Jesus* (Grand Rapids, MI: Revell, 2004), 26.

what pleases you. You desperately work to get to the point where you can say, "This is good enough. I bet God likes me now." If we're really honest with ourselves, the ultimate reason we want God to like us is because we think if He likes us, He will do what we want Him to do. More often than not, we think we can manipulate God to give us what we want.

However, the road of self-righteousness always has a deep ditch on either side of it. If you travel this road long enough, it will get so narrow that it will eventually push you into one ditch or the other. What are these two ditches? One is arrogance and the other is burnout, and they are equally dangerous.

The ditch of arrogance causes you to think you've reached super-Christian status. You have now been granted a capital *C* on your chest with a gold-plated shield around it. It will stay buried under the shirt of false humility, waiting for the perfect opportunity to bulge out. In these moments, you can show it off with how much theology you know, how many scriptures you can quote, and how you have an uncanny knack for pointing out others' specks through your plank-speared eyeballs. Yes, you've made it. You've reached the place of enlightenment. You're on the throne high and lifted up, and if people knew what was good for them, they would sit at your feet and soak up all your wisdom.

This is a dangerous ditch in which to find yourself because there's only one judge on all spiritual matters there—you. Whether it's the pastor's sermon or the lyrics to the latest song the worship band covered, nothing is deep enough for you. You're the smartest person in the room. You've got the inside track to the heart of God. However, deep down in your heart of hearts, you know it's all a sham. You're dying. You're fearful. You haven't heard the voice of God in ages, and you're beginning to hate the person you've become. Secret sins are ravaging your personal life, but on the outside, you look like the holy of holies. I believe the Pharisees, whom Jesus often criticized, operated the exact same way. You feel the pressure of knowing that others are starting to distance themselves from you, and you don't blame them, because it's all a facade—you can't stand yourself either. On top of it all, these all-too-sobering verses hang over your head:

> Pride goes before destruction,
> and a haughty spirit before a fall. (Proverbs 16:18)

> God opposes the proud but gives grace to the humble.
> (1 Peter 5:5)

If you don't fall into the ditch of arrogance, then the other ditch is sure to snatch you up. It is known as the ditch of burnout, and it is actually more like the ditch of arrogance than most would believe. Arrogance is a mask for insecurity, for feeling inadequate. Burnout is finally acknowledging your insecurity and inadequacy and then deciding to throw your hands up and say, "What's the point? I'll never measure up. I'll never have victory, so why even try? I quit."

Sadly, many great people have gotten stuck in this ditch, never to get out. Burnout has consumed far too many souls that were made for so much more. Ironically, many pastors and leaders fall into the ditch of burnout. Almost monthly, I personally hear of a pastor or ministry leader quitting and walking away from the ministry. Often in the midst of pouring into the lives of others, they find themselves empty. They start coasting on self-reliance and self-righteousness to continue. However, like my grandfather always said, "If you're coasting, then that means you're going downhill."

Far too many have rolled downhill by trying to get God to like them. Their downward momentum consisted of doing a lot of good things—so many that they coasted right into the ditch of burnout. Now they do nothing for God. They tried hard. They worked hard. And now they have nothing left to give. They're spiritually paralyzed. They can't move. They're suffering from spiritual lockjaw. They have nothing left to say.

People who have the scars and wounds of burnout have come face to face with the false belief of what I call if/then theology. *If* I do certain things for God, *then* He should do certain things for me. *If* I work hard to please Him, *then* He will work hard to please me. The moment God doesn't keep up His end of the bargain, I am one step closer to quitting and walking away.

Self-righteousness leaves a wake of people who are either so arrogant they don't need God anymore or so burned out they don't care about God anymore. And whether they realize it or not, it all started from a place of wanting God to like them.

Self-righteousness becomes its own form of religion, and religions are built on what mankind can do for their god or gods. However, the teachings of the Bible lead us in a very different direction. In fact, they lead us in the opposite direction. They don't lead to a ditch but to a life of freedom that can be found only in the love of God.

How Christianity Is the Exact Opposite
of Every World Religion

According to Wikipedia, there are an estimated 4,200 different religions and spiritual traditions in the world today.* These religions each derive their own set of morality, ethics, and religious laws from their distinct beliefs about the cosmos and human nature. Each one claims to be a superior way of experiencing life, and most maintain that their specific set of values came from a supernatural being, force, or power. Even though, by definition, all these religions contradict one another to a greater or lesser extent, our man-centered culture insists they're all valid and correct, pointing to the same God. "What is true for you isn't necessarily true for me" is the slogan of our culture. We're taught that an extreme tolerance of all these different viewpoints is our only option.

In a sense, tolerance has become the highest of all virtues in the world today. Now, a measure of tolerance is a good thing, in the sense that no one should be oppressed because of race, religion, or cultural differences, especially in daily interactions with people who profess beliefs different from one's own. However, the unfortunate truth is that our culture has taken tolerance to a completely unhealthy place; we no longer must simply tolerate but are forced to accept everyone else's belief systems, habits, and choices. We must affirm them as good, right, and just as acceptable as our own. In fact, our culture has become so tolerant that we're com-

---

* "List of Religions and Spiritual Traditions," Wikipedia, last modified July 31, 2018, 16:04, https://en.wikipedia.org/wiki/List_of_religions_and_spiritual_traditions.

pletely intolerant of anyone who says that someone or some group is wrong. That's what leads to ridiculous statements such as "We all worship the same God, just in different ways" or "All religions are the same; they're all headed to the same destination, just taking different paths."

However, deep down you know this doesn't sound right. How can they all be true if they all contradict one another? If one is true, then the others have to be lies, and if they are lies, then they're not helpful. They are not paths that lead to God but rather paths that lead to the ditches of self-righteousness and/or burnout.

This is where we must step in with gentle boldness and faithfully proclaim that not all religions are equally valid or true and that Christianity is the complete opposite of all of them. Right down to its core.

Allow me to take a moment to demonstrate what I mean by unpacking several of the more popular religions and the means by which a follower is taught to achieve the highest good within them.

Islam: According to the teachings of Islam, the purpose of life is to live in a way that is pleasing to Allah so that one may gain paradise. Islam teaches that at puberty, an account of each person's deeds is opened, and this account will be used on the day of judgment to determine the person's eternal fate. Essentially, in order to achieve salvation according to Islam, a person is required to express faith in Allah and in Muhammad, his prophet. Additionally, he must exhibit more good works than bad over the span of his life, from puberty through death. Many of the main characters in the origins of Islam are also found in the Bible. Hey, if you're going to plagiarize, the Bible is the best book to do it from. But you might as well just stick to studying the original source, right?

Buddhism: Religious beliefs are important in Buddhism, but its primary doctrines aren't necessarily the same as those of the other major world religions. For example, because Buddhism isn't monotheistic, or theistic at all really, it doesn't have doctrines about God. Nevertheless, certain beliefs are still central to the Buddhist worldview. Buddhists claim that these beliefs, summarized by the Four Noble Truths, enable them to free themselves from suffering by focusing on the beliefs instead of on the world around them. There is no generally understood salvation within Buddhism, only an eternal end to suffering achieved by not chasing after things that do not give lasting happiness. The end goal is to achieve Nirvana upon death. Some of the most dedicated and disciplined people I know are Buddhists. In fact, one of their regular disciplines is fasting, which I personally find ironic when I see the statue of Buddha.

Hinduism: This ancient Eastern religion embraces a diversity of beliefs, a fact that can be confusing to those accustomed to a Western religious practice that has creeds, confessions, and carefully worded belief statements. One can believe a variety of things about the divine, the universe, and the path to liberation and still be considered a Hindu. Perhaps the most well-known Hindu saying about religion is "Truth is one; sages call it by different names." Still, there are some beliefs common to nearly all forms of Hinduism, which form the boundaries of what may be properly called

Hinduism. These include the authority of the ancient Indian sacred texts, the Brahmins (priests), reincarnation, and the law of Karma (or the right or wrong that one does). These core beliefs determine one's destiny both in this life and the next. Furthermore, most Hindus are followers of one of the principal gods (there are technically over one million recognized gods in Hinduism!). The principal gods are known as Shiva, Vishnu, and Brahma, though these are all considered to be manifestations of a single reality. If there is a teaching in this particular religion that is extremely interesting to me, it's reincarnation. Obviously, I don't hold to this teaching. However, there are a few people I'd like to see come back to earth as a dung beetle, a platypus, or even a *Tyrannosaurus rex*. Think about how frustrating it must be to have such a big body with tiny arms!

Judaism: Right doctrine and theology are very important in Judaism. To arrive at a right system of beliefs, the Hebrew Scriptures address the biggest topics in life—from God to the universe to human nature. It is vital for a devout follower of Judaism to believe the testimony of these Scriptures. Judaism is also different from other ancient Near Eastern religions in the belief that God is unitary and solitary; thus, His relationships are not with other gods or deities but with humans, whom He created. Judaism can be described primarily as ethical monotheism—the belief that God is one, that He is concerned with the actions of mankind, and that the actions of mankind (namely, following or disobeying God's commandments) are the primary means by which a follower of Judaism may obtain eternal life. Hebrew is the historical language of the Jews, and it's an absolutely beautiful script. However, don't ever get a Hebrew tattoo unless you absolutely know and understand the language. I may or may not have made this mistake personally.

Confucianism: This religion concentrates on appropriate behavior in life, not a future heaven. The afterlife is unknowable, so all effort should be made to make this life the best it can be, to honor ancestors, and to respect elders. The purpose of life is to fulfill one's role in society with propriety, honor, and loyalty. I've tried to study and understand this religion, but I've just found myself completely . . . are you ready? Confused.

Scientology: For Scientologists, the true self is the spirit or thetan, the eternal essence of each individual. For millions and millions of years prior to this life, the thetan has existed and has inhabited numerous bodies. The process of moving on and being reborn as a baby in a new body occurs as a natural and normal part of the universe. Thus, Scientology's understanding of the process of the afterlife is very much in accord with Hinduism in many respects, except for the idea of Karma, or a moral judgment based on the previous life of the soul. Adherents of Scientology look forward to their next embodied life and the ultimate goal of taking the truth of Scientology to all people. Scientology founder L. Ron Hubbard famously stated, "You don't get rich writing science fiction. If you want to get rich, you start a religion." Well, his created religion made him a very, very wealthy man. Yet when you google his name, one of the most popular hits that pops up is the statement "L. Ron Hubbard's teeth." Sadly, he will be forever known as someone with bad doctrine and bad teeth.

Jehovah's Witnesses: They believe that they are Christian and that there are different levels of heaven. The anointed are 144,000 who receive salvation by the blood of Christ and will rule with Him in paradise. They are the bride of Christ. For all others, Jesus's sacrifice freed them only from Adam's curse of original sin, and faith is merely the opportunity to earn their way to heaven. They must learn about kingdom history, keep the laws of Jehovah, and be loyal to "God's government"—the 144,000 leaders, 9,000 of whom are currently on the earth. They must also spread the news about the kingdom through door-to-door proselytizing. After they die, they will be resurrected during the millennial kingdom, where they must continue a devout life. Only afterward will they be given the opportunity to formally accept Christ and live for eternity under the rule of the 144,000 leaders. Now you know the beliefs of the people who are standing on your front porch as you're pretending not to be at home.

Mormonism: Unlike Christianity, Mormonism espouses a distinctly nontrinitarian theology in regard to the Father, Son, and Holy Ghost. Mormons believe they are three physically separate and distinct beings, though one in thought, action, and purpose. Mormonism teaches that God the Father is literally the father of the spirits of all men and women, which existed prior to their mortal existence. Further, all humans, as children of God, can become exalted, inheriting all that God has and becoming like Him as a god. The primary means by which Mormons believe one may live eternally and be exalted is through a combination of faith and good works, with an emphasis on good works. There is also special underwear that is to be worn during certain ceremo-nies. I grew up in the country, so for me, holy underwear meant something totally different. Typically, it meant it was time to make a trip to the nearest Walmart for a new pair.

As is readily apparent, all these religions have plenty of differ-ences in their teachings and in the views of their deity, or lack thereof. However, every religion basically espouses a very similar practice when it comes to the creatures trying to figure out how to please their deity (or deities). Each one boils down to the creatures trying to get their god or gods to like them.

These religions are all about creation reaching up and trying to attain the state or quality of their ultimate beings and holding on for dear (eternal) life. Possibly, if you reach up high enough, your god will accept you. If your deity accepts and likes you, then surely he will do what you want him to, right? Everything will go your way.

However, biblical Christianity teaches the exact opposite of all these other major religions. Ultimately, there is nothing we can do—nothing that makes us good enough or nice enough. There are not enough beads in the world to count. There is no amount of money that can purchase God's favor. There are no chants or prayers loud enough. There is no enlightenment for us apart from Christ because we're actually born spiritually dead, and no matter what we do or don't do, this deity will not and cannot accept us in our fallen human nature. "You were dead in the trespasses and sins in which you once walked" (Ephesians 2:1–2). Dead people have no ability to get God to like them.

Therefore, unlike all other religions, Christianity teaches that we don't have to try to reach up to God. We don't have to work really hard to get God to like us, because our great God already loves us. Instead of us reaching up to Him, God Himself reached down to us. He took on the form and nature of His creation in the person of Jesus, without ceasing to be God, and then died a substitutionary, sacrificial death to atone for the sins of His own creation. After this sacrificial death, Jesus was raised to life in order to demonstrate that He was God and that His death was sufficient payment for the sin of mankind. Jesus doesn't merely point us to the way of eternal life, but He Himself is the way to eternal life. Faith in Jesus as the atoning sacrifice for sin is the only requirement of Christianity. There is no level of spiritual enlightenment we must attain or number of good works we must perform in order to be accepted by God. He has already done everything necessary for us to be redeemed and offered salvation through faith in Jesus. In other words, mankind can be saved by a good work . . . just not ours. Rather, it is the good work of Jesus on our behalf. "By grace you have been saved through faith. And this is not your own doing; it is the gift of God, not a result of works, so that no one may boast" (Ephesians 2:8–9).

The Father is very fond of us. That is the exact opposite of every other religion in the world! Besides Christianity, found in the New Testament, no other system of belief teaches how great the Father's love is for us. It is beautiful. It is perfect. It is life changing.

The Beauty and Freedom
of God's Unconditional Love

See, my friend Jeff at the Christian summer camp (who was working really hard to be a good person and was trying to get God to like him) was actually practicing his own form of religion, something completely opposite of what the Bible teaches about being a follower of Jesus. He was enslaved by a common lie instead of enjoying the freedom of a very unique God.

God operates with a different love than we do. He is motivated by and acts upon His agape love for His creation. *Agape* is a Greek word for an ultimate self-sacrificing kind of love. Agape love is the kind that is always associated with the love of God and the way He extends that perfect love toward His creation. It's a type of love that we'll never know or experience apart from God. We can't get it from others, because a natural human kind of love falls way short of agape love. Most relationships are built on an if/then kind of love, better known as conditional love. If you do what I want you to do, then I will love you. If you love me, then I will love you back. In contrast, God's love is unconditional. He loves us even when we mess up. He has the ability to love those who do not even love Him back.

This kind of love can come only from an all-loving heavenly Father. The Greek word *agape* was hardly ever used in Greek-speaking societies, but in the New Testament it occurs 320 times. It is a love that God extended to us when we didn't deserve it. He gives it to us and doesn't expect us to pay it back, because we never could. It is truly an unconditional kind of love. "God shows his

love for us in that while we were still sinners, Christ died for us"
(Romans 5:8).

You don't have to try really hard to get God to like you, because He already deeply, perfectly, unconditionally loves you. He
loved you before you ever had a chance to do things for Him. In
fact, He loved you before you ever knew Him. He even loved you
before He created you. Take a minute to wrap your mind around
that little nugget of truth. You think God doesn't care about you?
He loved you before He created you! "He chose us in him before
the foundation of the world, that we should be holy and blameless
before him. In love he predestined us for adoption to himself as
sons through Jesus Christ, according to the purpose of his will"
(Ephesians 1:4–5).

Wow! How amazing is this love? Words escape us when we
try to describe it. It's one thing to love your spouse, your children,
and those who love you back. But what about loving someone
who could never love you back equally? What about loving
someone who doesn't deserve it or maybe didn't even want it at the
time you extended it? What about loving someone in a way that
would cost you everything, even your only child? This is the agape
love that the Father has for you.

This type of love is what was displayed on the cross of Jesus
Christ. It was the type of love I was preaching about at that West
Texas camp in the middle of July, when we looked at the beauty
of John 3:16: "For God so loved the world, that he gave his only
Son, that whoever believes in him should not perish but have eternal life." It is the type of love that Ed Farrell's uncle knew quite
well. But sadly, this is the type of love that Jeff was completely

missing out on because he was too busy trying to get God to like him. The sobering truth about this kind of love is that you can't do both. You can't work to get God to like you and at the same time rest in the fact that He already loves you. Eventually one will conquer the other. Hopefully, at some point, the power of God's love will overwhelm you to the point that you would never settle for God merely liking you. Strive for more. Don't settle until you settle in the depths of the Father's love for you. And there you will discover that, yes, the Father is very fond of you!

Questions for Common Lie 8

1. Tell about a time in your life when you were so busy trying to get God to like you that you neglected to enjoy the truth that He already loves you.

2. According to this chapter, what are the two ditches of self-righteousness? In the moments of life when you're not focusing on Christ, which ditch do you tend to slip into—arrogance or burnout?

3. Of the world religions described in the section titled "How Christianity Is the Exact Opposite of Every World Religion," which one are you the least familiar with? Do you know people who practice these religions? If so, which ones? What words would you use to describe those people?

4. What is the main difference between what other religions teach about salvation and what the gospel teaches?

5. Read Ephesians 2:8–9 and John 3:16. What does *agape* mean? Is that understanding of love foreign or familiar to you?

A Truth to Move Forward With

You can't work to get God to like you and at the same time rest in the fact that God already loves you. You have to choose.

Believe in Yourself

Sorry, Rock, But . . .

Guess what? I've seen all the Rocky movies. And when I say all, I mean all, even the one where Rock fought Tommy Gunn (yeah, that one was pretty bad). What's more is that I've seen them more than once, and I'm proud to admit it. They are fantastic movies that never fail to stir the fire in me. *Rocky Balboa* was released in 2006, and with it came easily one of the most inspirational speeches ever given by the Italian Stallion. The speech occurs on a sidewalk late in the evening, and the audience for these moving words is his son:

> Let me tell you something you already know. The world
> ain't all sunshine and rainbows. It's a very mean and nasty
> place, and I don't care how tough you are, it will beat you
> to your knees and keep you there permanently if you let it.
> You, me, or nobody is gonna hit as hard as life. But it ain't
> about how hard you hit. It's about how hard you can get

hit and keep moving forward. How much you can take and keep moving forward. That's how winning is done! Now if you know what you're worth then go out and get what you're worth. But ya gotta be willing to take the hits, and not pointing fingers saying you ain't where you wanna be because of him, or her, or anybody! Cowards do that and that ain't you! You're better than that! I'm always gonna love you no matter what. No matter what happens. You're my son and you're my blood. You're the best thing in my life. But until you start believing in yourself, ya ain't gonna have a life.

Man, I love that. It makes me want to drink a raw egg or two, work a speed bag, and then go conquer the world or something. There is so much gold in that speech. But as the phrase goes, "All that glitters is not gold." As much as I love that speech, there's a line in there that's much more than just a line. It's a lie (sorry, Rock).

"Believe in yourself!" How many times have we been given this line as a pep talk? I really believe this is shared with the best of intentions. It is a banner statement in our new tradition of building up the self-esteem of a new generation. For nearly thirty years now, it has been an accepted fact in psychology that low self-esteem is the root of many social and personal problems, particularly among young people. Low self-esteem is to blame for everything, from the high school drop-out rate to teenage pregnancy, from overflowing prisons to suicides, from drug abuse to hate crimes. If we can change how people view themselves, we can help change how they act. If people believe they are winners, then they will be winners. "That's how winning is done!"

Don't get me wrong. The self-esteem movement has the right motivation behind it, but not the right message. Of course we all want to feel good about ourselves. None of us want to live with low self-esteem, nor do we want our children to dislike themselves. However, the evidence is overwhelming: increased self-esteem hasn't helped. Our children grow up to see how empty participation trophies are. Prisons are still full. Drug abuse, violence, and suicides are never in short supply. In fact, most people agree that things are simply getting worse.

Our culture continues to tell us that the greatest attribute is the ability to take matters into your own hands—to be the determiner of your own destiny and the captain of your own ship. You can do anything you set your mind to. Believe and achieve! Pull yourself up by your own bootstraps. There are whole sections of bookstores devoted to helping you have self-confidence above all else and to rely on yourself alone.

This kind of advice resonates with our human nature because at the end of the day, we all love taking matters into our own hands. We'd rather trust in ourselves because it makes us feel in control. Deep down, however, in the true essence of who we are, in our soul and spirit, we know it's a lie. The truth is, the older you get, the more you begin to realize that one of your greatest enemies is yourself. No one has misled you more than you've misled yourself. No one has lied to you more than you've lied to yourself. No one has hurt, distracted, or hindered you more than you have. In fact, the more you believe in yourself, the deeper the pit you find yourself in. Have you ever noticed that the harder you try, the more you mess up?

As good as it sounds, "Believe in yourself" is a lie. Don't believe in yourself. Believe in Someone bigger than yourself, knowing that same Someone will give you a power that causes you to live differently everywhere you go throughout your life. "You will receive power when the Holy Spirit has come upon you, and you will be my witnesses in Jerusalem and in all Judea and Samaria, and to the end of the earth" (Acts 1:8).

The Bible offers numerous clear warnings about why you shouldn't believe in yourself. Here are three biggies.

Believing in Self Caused the Fall of the Human Race

The serpent (Lucifer) tempted Adam and Eve with the very same thing that got him booted out of heaven, telling them, in essence, "You can and will be like God. There is no reason to trust God any longer because you can be like God yourself." "For God knows that when you eat of it your eyes will be opened, and you will be like God, knowing good and evil" (Genesis 3:5). This was the great temptation in the Garden of Eden. It was more than taking a bite of fruit. It was mankind wanting to be God, listening to the serpent over their creator, and believing in themselves more than trusting God's direction.

Believing in Self Caused Problems for the Israelites in the Old Testament

God continually accused the Israelites of doing whatever was right in their own eyes instead of trusting in Him. "In those days there was no king in Israel. Everyone did what was right in his own eyes" (Judges 17:6). The people didn't need God because they believed the same statement we believe today: "To each his own." They believed in themselves and felt no need to believe in God for direction.

Believing in Self Is the Opposite of What Jesus Taught

The fundamental statement that Jesus gave us about following Him was not for us to believe in ourselves but rather the exact opposite—to deny ourselves. This denial is more than letting go of some dream or desire. The call is to deny our whole selves, all our natural motives and impulses that conflict with the claims of Christ. In fact, He went even further to say that we must take up our cross, which is an instrument of death. So are we supposed to believe in ourselves? No, actually we're supposed to die to ourselves! "Jesus told His disciples, 'If anyone would come after me, let him deny himself and take up his cross and follow me'" (Matthew 16:24). Jesus was talking about a different way to live. Actually, it's not just a *different* way from what is natural to the world. It's an *opposite* way.

The Paradox of the Gospel

When the apostle Paul described the gospel in comparison to the world, he said, "The word of the cross is folly to those who are perishing, but to us who are being saved it is the power of God" (1 Corinthians 1:18). To the non-Christian, the story of a God coming to earth to die for His people so they wouldn't have to depend on themselves seems absolutely foolish. There is a way that seems right to most people. The systems of the world and the structures of success are built around trusting in yourself instead of someone else. In fact, if your main goal in life is to trust in someone else, you'll most likely be labeled as lazy, dependent, and weak. After all, isn't the trick to get all you can, in any way you can? Step on whomever you can, and do it while you still can? You better believe in yourself and do it yourself, because no one else is going to do it for you.

Paul, in this same chapter of 1 Corinthians, continued to teach the opposite of this when he said, "Where is the one who is wise? Where is the scribe? Where is the debater of this age? Has not God made the foolish the wisdom of the world? For since, in the wisdom of God, the world did not know God through wisdom, it pleased God through the folly of what we preach to save those who believe" (verses 20–21). God chooses to give us freedom, victory, and success in ways opposite of what would seem natural to us. It's what I like to call the paradox of the gospel.

According to the *Merriam-Webster Dictionary,* the word *paradox* means "a tenet contrary to received opinion" or "a statement that is seemingly contradictory or opposed to common sense and yet is perhaps true." Basically, what seems foolish in the eyes of most of our friends, family, and coworkers who don't have a relationship with God is often the thing that is most important to us. What seems silly to the world is the very thing that ushers in the power of God. When you compare the principles of God's way of doing things to the principles of the world's way of doing things, everything will seem backward. Up is down. Left is right.

Wrong is right. A bull's-eye doesn't even hit the target. Gaining is losing. Last is first. And living is dying.

Here are a few prime examples of scriptural paradoxes:

- *To be exalted, you must be humbled.* "Humble yourselves before the Lord, and he will exalt you" (James 4:10). "Humble yourselves, therefore, under the mighty hand of God so that at the proper time he may exalt you" (1 Peter 5:6). Every day, God does extraordinary things through ordinary people who believe in Him. He chooses to use people who healthily place others before themselves. Are you doing things for God and others, or is everything you're doing motivated by selfish ambitions? He will often bring down those who try to exalt themselves and will often exalt those who humble themselves.

- *To be strong, you must be weak.* "He said to me, 'My grace is sufficient for you, for my power is made perfect in weakness.' Therefore I will boast all the more gladly of my weaknesses, so that the power of Christ may rest upon me. For the sake of Christ, then, I am content with weaknesses, insults, hardships, persecutions, and calamities. For when I am weak, then I am strong" (2 Corinthians 12:9–10). Often, when we think we're at our strongest, we will by default depend on ourselves. When you're depending on yourself, you'll never have the strength to endure the hardships that life throws your way. However, when you are utterly dependent on the Lord, you will stand strong in the midst of storms because you are standing on the rock—Jesus. You are at your best when you're most dependent on Him. The power of Christ is most visible in you when you're able to be faithful in spite of sicknesses, trials, troubles, and circumstances.

- *To be a receiver, you must be a giver.* "In all things I have shown you that by working hard in this way we must help the weak and remember the words of the Lord Jesus, how he himself said, 'It is more blessed to give than to receive'" (Acts 20:35). The common philosophy practiced by most is "It's better to work as much as you can, earn all you can, save it all, get very rich, keep it for yourself, and withhold from others if you have to so that your children can fight over it once they lower you into a six-foot grave." The irony is that some of the most miserable people in the world are those who take from others, while some of the most joyful people in the world are those who give unselfishly. God is more generous than any person on earth, and if He is living inside you, He will change you to become more and more like Him. When you give your time, talents, and treasures to God for the good of others, you will receive some of the greatest gifts of all—joy, peace, satisfaction, and fulfillment. If you have been given those things, then you're truly rich indeed.

- *To gain, you must lose.* "Whatever gain I had, I counted as loss for the sake of Christ. Indeed, I count everything as loss because of the surpassing worth of knowing Christ Jesus my Lord. For his sake I have suffered the loss of all things and count them as rubbish, in order that I may gain Christ" (Philippians 3:7–8). So many times we are too busy chasing after good things, such as money, relationships, career, and prestige, that we completely miss out on the greatest gift of all—Christ. For example, money in and of itself is not bad. However, when we love it more than God and people, it becomes evil. "The love of money is a root of all kinds of evils. It is through this craving that some have wandered away from the faith and pierced themselves with many pangs" (1 Timothy 6:10). It's our drive of wanting and gaining more stuff that often causes us not to pursue the Savior. It's scary to think that we can gain it all—everything the world has to offer—and lose the very essence of who we are, our souls. Things will never truly satisfy us. We'll always need and want more. The paradox of the gospel is that after gaining, we are to live a life of service and sacrifice for Him. Only then can we be truly satisfied. The world may think we're losers for losing what's rightfully ours, but we will have the freedom of knowing we have gained victory in Christ. Gaining Him is gaining the fulfillment that our souls long for.

- *To live, you must die.* "If you live according to the flesh you will die, but if by the Spirit you put to death the deeds of the body, you will live" (Romans 8:13). There is a popular saying, YOLO, which means, "you only live once." A lot of people use this as a mantra for conquest. To make the most out of life, get the most money, the most accolades, or the most sexual partners. Sadly, you can live it up in this life while being marked for an eternity separated from God. It is true that you only live once, and then comes forever—either with God or away from God. There is no in-between. To truly live, to truly know joy, to truly experience all this world was created for is to know the One by whom it was created. Jesus is the life, and to have this life you must die to yourself. The more you die to self, the more life is in you because Christ is in you! "He must increase, but I must decrease" (John 3:30). "If Christ is in you, although the body is dead because of sin, the Spirit is life because of righteousness" (Romans 8:10).

How incredibly confusing, and yet so wonderfully beautiful, are these paradoxes of the gospel. The kingdom of God operates in a way that is the exact opposite of everything that seems natural to living in this world today. Solomon, one of the wisest men to ever live, said, "There is a way that seems right to a man, but its end is the way to death" (Proverbs 14:12). How wild! Living in the freedom of the paradoxes of the gospel feels unnatural, abnormal, and, frankly, absolutely crazy. Maybe that is why it takes so much faith.

The Pressure's Off

In my late twenties, I decided I was going to take up the sport of boxing. A guy in our church was a boxing coach and ran his own gym. One day I approached my wife and proclaimed to her that I believed God was calling me to start boxing as a hobby. (That was the superspiritual way I would approach my wife with things I really wanted to do but knew she would think were silly: "God called me.") Don't get me wrong. My wife has been incredibly supportive of every crazy thing I have dreamed up over the years and has pretty much encouraged me to do anything I've ever wanted to do. Believe me, there are a lot of wacky ideas that come out of this brain. I have one of those personalities. I will gravitate to a new hobby, go all in on it, get all the gear that comes with my newfound passion, and then move on to a new hobby within months. Know anyone like that? Yep, that's me. My garage is full of things I've purchased for the hobbies I believed God "called me" to do, and I can imagine Him on His throne saying, "Pruitt, don't blame Me for that."

Boxing was my new hobby at the time. I told my wife, "Babe, I can do this. I'll be in great shape, and at the same time I can disciple the church member who is going to train me." (That was another superspiritual rationalization in my arsenal for taking up boxing—I can "disciple" him.) So my boxing career began. After training three days a week for about two months, I felt great. I was probably in the best shape of my life. I believed in my misguided brain that I was very similar to Rocky in his prime. So I explained to my trainer that I was ready to get in the ring to spar with someone. Sparring is not a full-on boxing match, where you are trying to knock the other person's head off. Rather, it is meant for practice, swinging at each other with about 50 percent of your full power.

My trainer, in all his graciousness, strongly advised against this, saying, "You don't want to do that. You're just training to get in shape and have fun. Plus, the only other person here right now is Tony. You don't need to get in the ring with Tony. He is now a pro boxer." Come on. What did he know? I'd been boxing for two months, and my trainer had been doing this for only a short twenty years. And Tony? He was a featherweight, which means he weighed between 118 and 126 pounds. "Listen, my boxing guru, I weigh 210 pounds. I have almost 100 pounds on him. Don't worry. I will take it easy on him." Gosh, what an idiot I was. Tony was a featherweight Golden Gloves winner, which basically means he was a champion and it was a very, very bad idea to get in the ring with him. But there we were, gloves on, helmets on, and mouthpieces in our mouths. We stepped to the middle and touched gloves, just like the real thing. Tony informed me he would just move around and let me try to hit him. To which I replied with a hurt ego, "See these eyes? Eyes of the tiger, man. You better give me all you got because I am coming for you with all 200 pounds of this muscle." (It was actually very little muscle.)

Here is the highlight of my boxing career, as best I can recall, because my memory is still a little hazy. I walked to him and reared back to give him a punch that his great-grandmamma would feel. However, before I could do anything, a tiny featherweight fist hit me square in the face, and it felt like a bomb went off as soon as it connected. I remember a bright flash of light, my knees going weak, and then an up-close meeting with the mat of the boxing ring. And that was it. My boxing career was over. Unlike Rocky, there would be no Pruitt II or III or IV or V. That day I retired from boxing. I hung up my gloves. I was in over my head. This was way over my pay grade. God was now calling me to stick to preaching the Bible and to leave the boxing to Tony. Tony was built to be a boxer, and it's now his job. I was not built to be a boxer. That is not God's best for me. It's not what I was created to do. And, just like it is not my job to be a boxer, it is also not my job to be in control.

At the core of believing in ourselves is our desire to be in control. However, if you attempt to live life believing in yourself, you will be trapped by discouragement, fear, anxiety, and worry. The pressure of trying to be in control of all situations will set you up to be eventually knocked out by the hardships of life. Living in this world can pack a punch that may put you on the mat, but it can't move God off His throne. You were not made to believe in yourself, because you were not made to be in control. You were made to believe in Someone else. You were made to trust Someone else to be in control. That is ultimately what faith is—trusting in the One who sits on the throne as king.

There is wonderful freedom in living this way. It takes all the pressure off you and places it on the One who can handle it. A great thing about believing in God and trusting Him with your life is that He does not struggle with the same things you and I do. He never gets stressed, anxious, or worried. He is in control of all things, has a plan and purpose, and is strong enough to see it through. We will fail. He never does. We will make mistakes. He never does. We will make a mess of things. He never does. He can be trusted. Time and time again He has proven Himself. But to believe in Him means we have to let go. Letting go means we can no longer hold on to it. Whatever that "it" is for you, it's time to place it in the hands of God and let go of it. Faith steps in the moment you let go.

Most people don't realize that Sylvester Stallone (Rocky) actually wrote the Rocky movies. If I were to rewrite Rocky's motivational speech from the beginning of this chapter to share with my own kids in hopes that it would help prepare them for this crazy journey called life, it would go something like this:

> Let me tell you something you may or may not already know. The world ain't all sunshine and rainbows. In fact, sometimes it's storms and floods. Then there are other times that it's scorching heat and droughts. It's a very mean and nasty place, and I don't care how tough you are, it will beat you to your knees and keep you there permanently if you try to take on this world by your own strength and power. There are two great enemies that we must face—the devil and the person you look at in the mirror every day. The devil wants to kill, steal, and destroy you. He is not after the world. He already has that. He

wants you. He hates what God loves—you. When that enemy is not messing with you, then the enemy you look at every day in the mirror will be. Besides the devil, no one is going to set you up for failure more than you will. Nobody is gonna hit as hard as this fallen world will.

But it ain't about how hard you hit back, because you will continue to let yourself down time and time again. It's about how hard your God can take a hit, because He that is in you is greater than he that is in the world. When you want to give up, God's power never runs out. When you want to hide, God shows up and shows out. When you want to retreat, God keeps moving forward. That's how winning is done! His victory becomes your victory. That's all that matters, and it will matter forever and ever!

Now, God has bought you with the blood of His own Son, Jesus, and there is nothing more valuable than that. Do you know what you're worth? Your value is immeasurable. Not because of how awesome you are but because of how awesome your Jesus is! So go out and get all the spiritual riches that Christ has bought for you. Don't settle. Don't compromise. You are a child of the King! The King of all kings.

But you gotta be willing to surrender, to give up, to die. Die to yourself, and find the life called Jesus. Cowards don't do that. They're scared to let go. It takes real faith to trust Jesus with everything. So we hold on. We want to be in control. And we try and try and try. Until the day we finally realize that the harder we try, the more we mess up.

But you're better than that! Or, better yet, your Jesus is better than that.

I'm always gonna love you no matter what. No matter what happens. You're my child and you're my blood. Besides Jesus and your momma, you're the best thing in my life. But until you stop believing in yourself, ya ain't gonna have a life, because life is found in a person named Jesus. He loves you more than I can. He bought you with His blood. You belong to Him. Make sure you live in a way that tells the world that He is the best thing in your life. And the best way to do that is by making a daily decision to not believe in yourself, but rather to believe in Him.

Questions for Common Lie 9

1. What do you think most people mean when they use the statement "Believe in yourself"?

2. According to this chapter, what are one or two problems that believing in yourself causes?

3. Read Matthew 16:24. What is Jesus asking you to do? What are the main differences between believing in yourself and denying yourself?

4. In the section titled "The Paradox of the Gospel," which paradox encouraged you the most? How can focusing on this boost your spiritual growth?

5. What areas of your life do you try to control? How's that going? Why do you think it's so hard to trust God to be in control of every area of your life? What is one thing in your life—just one—that you can turn over to God this week?

A Truth to Move Forward With

You don't have to live with the pressure of believing in yourself when you fully trust God to be in control.

Handicapped and Healed

The Handicapped Ones

I know it has been a while. Maybe you zipped through this book in a couple of weeks, or perhaps your reading style is much like mine—read a couple of chapters, get distracted with other things, read a few more chapters, and get distracted again. So maybe it's been weeks or even months since you read the introduction. Whatever the case, I wrapped up the intro by talking about one of the greatest gifts in my life, my son Titus. I'd like to close out the book in the same way, talking about Titus.

Several years ago, there was an incident that happened to Kasi that ended up changing both our perspectives forever. She was visiting a Bible study at a local church and had checked Titus into the room where child care was being provided. It was a bustling place, full of noise and busy toddlers. After the Bible study was over, Kasi returned to the room to pick up Titus. With a smile on her face, she said to one of the adult workers, "Wow, you all have your hands full today." The worker replied, "Yes, we do, and now we have a handicapped one." The look on the worker's face gave her away. She viewed our son as a burden. After Kasi picked her chin up off the ground, she responded to the woman, "Yes, I know. He is mine." The worker did a double take. She obviously had no idea the little dark-skinned boy in a wheelchair was the son of the light-skinned blond girl. She mumbled a few more things as Kasi got our son out of there as quickly as possible.

Walking away from that room, my beautiful wife had tears running down her face. Tears of anger. Tears of sadness. Tears of honesty. By this time, Kasi had reached a healthy place of facing her own sadness head-on. Her sadness over the physical suffering of our son, and her sadness over others who suffer from ignorance. That poor lady had no idea that Kasi was his mom, and Kasi completely understood that. However, on many levels, that made the incident much, much worse. Our son, who was adopted from Uganda when he was six months old, is the most easygoing little man you will ever meet. He is always smiling and always happy. And because Kasi knows this without a doubt, there was no way this child-care worker could convince her that he would in any way be a burden as he sat in that room for approximately an hour.

As the day went on, Kasi couldn't shake what was said. She shared the story with me, and it made both of us extremely sad that this is how some people view our son. They see him only as "the handicapped one," and so he is considered a burden to everyone around him. Wow, how could someone view our precious boy as a burden?

Well, if we were to be honest, there was a time shortly after adopting him when we felt the same way. When Kasi and I started the process of adoption, we were open only to a completely healthy little boy. We didn't think that with our lifestyle we would be able to handle a child with special needs. We were unaware of the severity of our little man's needs when we first brought him home, but we soon found out they were much more than we had anticipated. We struggled for a long while. *How could God let this happen to us? What have we done? Did we make a mistake? Can we handle this?* These were all questions we asked ourselves on the inside but were not brave enough to express out loud. Sadly, there were times when it was all a heavy burden. Instead of being honest with our feelings and taking them to the truth of God's Word, we masked and suppressed them with nice-sounding one-liners that were not even biblically true.

There will be times when God will gently—or not so gently—start showing you that His plan is far greater than anything you could have imagined for yourself. He "is able to do far more abundantly than all that we ask or think, according to the power at work within us" (Ephesians 3:20). For us, God used a little boy to expose some deep-rooted sin in our lives that we didn't even realize was there.

Pride and the American dream were idols we had cuddled up to without even knowing it. We wanted the picture-perfect family and would not settle for anything less in our own estimation. This led to some other sins we held on to ever so tightly. Arrogance and entitlement had become our close friends, even though we never would have admitted it. Kasi and I were doing a good thing by adopting, so surely God would give us the perfect little baby boy we had pictured in our minds. After all, our happiness is most important, right? (Thankfully, we have already exposed that lie.) What about the idol of comfort? Well, comfort had become what we deeply longed for. We wanted to adopt, but we were entering adoption on our own terms. We didn't want to be stretched. We wanted the easy route. We wanted to be comfortable.

"The handicapped one." "The handicapped one." "The handicapped one." As we continued to think about that statement over and over and over again, we recognized it for what it was and is—a lie. Our son Titus is not the handicapped one. Now, don't get me wrong. Obviously he is in a wheelchair, but that isn't *who* he is. Titus is a beautiful boy, made in the image of a God who makes no mistakes, and he is the bravest person I've ever met. He is an encouragement to all those around him, and his smile is downright contagious. He is the epitome of joy, peace, and love. And he pushes me to be a better man, husband, daddy, and follower of Jesus.

Our son, although in a wheelchair, is not the handicapped one. On the contrary, we were the handicapped ones. Before Titus came into our lives, Kasi and I were handicapped by so many things. We felt that God owed us something because we were "good people." On top of that, we were in ministry. Oh yes, I bet God was impressed with us. Gross, right? It almost makes me sick to my stomach to look back and think about those days. I'm certain there were many times when God rolled His eyes at us in response to our way of thinking.

As Titus has grown older and we have continued to walk the winding road of special-needs parenting, we have become more and more thankful that God did not listen to our little self-centered prayers. Well, maybe He did listen, but thankfully, He didn't answer them the way we wanted Him to, because He knew better. God, in His all-knowing power, certainly knew what we needed more than we did. Our son's seizures have broken us of our pride. His endless doctor's appointments have shattered our arrogance. His never-ending therapy has blown our entitlement right out of the water. And dealing nonstop with insurance companies and hospital stays, well, that has for sure stripped away a lot of our comforts.

This little boy, who has never spoken a word, can't feed himself, can't walk, and is dependent on us for every single need, is an instrument used by God on a daily basis. He lights up the room. He is a fighter. He has to work every day to do what is considered normal by most people. He is handsome, and he is beautiful, inside and out. And he is a downright miracle. Although he is made uniquely, he is still fearfully and wonderfully made. "I praise you, for I am fearfully and wonderfully made. Wonderful are your works; my soul knows it very well" (Psalm 139:14).

God Sets You Free by His Truth, Not the Lies of Pithy One-Liners

The bottom line is that we live in a fallen world, a world that is cursed by sin. But in the midst of this world sits our son—a gift we never expected. Through this gift, God has taught us to be thankful for the smallest things, not only in our son's life, but also in the lives of our other children. God has taught us to slow down and cherish each and every day. We used to constantly look to the future, worrying through the questions *What will be next? What is around the corner?* "But seek first the kingdom of God and his righteousness, and all these things will be added to you. Therefore do not be anxious about tomorrow, for tomorrow will be anxious for itself. Sufficient for the day is its own trouble" (Matthew 6:33–34). We had been doing more worrying than seeking. However, with Titus, the thought of the future can be downright scary. So in light of this, we have learned to focus on seeking the Lord each day, to be thankful for each and every moment, and to let tomorrow's worries worry about themselves.

Our heavenly Father has also used Titus to constantly remind us that this life is but a moment, and a fleeting one at that. We pray for healing for our boy all the time, but the amazing reality is that one day healing will happen for Titus. It may or may not be in our timing, but it will come, either on this earth or in eternity. Healing will happen, and it will happen completely. We worship a healing God who makes the impossible possible.

Also, God had to put to death the picture-perfect family we had imagined for the Pruitt household, the family for whom everything went the way we wanted it to go. He had to bury that, and we had to let Him, in faith. Honestly, we went through a season of grieving and letting go of this ideal image of a perfectly healthy baby that we had been asking and waiting for. We had to realize that God's plan for us was so much better than our own. See, as much as we like to think that we are in control, the fact is we're not. When you realize that God's ways are so much better than your own, you'll find a peace that is indescribable. You'll be free to trust Him and to rest in the truth that He knows what you need more than you do.

Although we had to put to death what we thought we wanted, God brought us a life we couldn't have dreamed of. Is it easy? Nope. Do we have hard days? Absolutely. Do we have days of being completely overwhelmed, where God gives us more than we can handle? A big yes! But Titus is worth every bit of it.

Titus has also taught us more than we could ever have imagined about the depth of love that our great God has for us. It amazes me how Jesus can look at me and see all my pride, anxiety, selfishness, and sin and yet still love me, still forgive me, and still choose to adopt me as His own! In some small way, that's how we see Titus. We no longer see the seizures, physical and mental delays, fear of the unknown, or special needs. We see our son—our son we would do anything for, our son whom we wouldn't trade for a healthy or normally developed child, even if given the option. Having Titus in our family has caused us to be even more aware of and in awe of the incredible love that God has for every one of His children.

Although we don't always understand what God is doing, we can trust that He knows best. So goodbye, picture-perfect family. Now that I think about it, what does that even look like? To us, it is exactly what the Lord has given us. Our family is not perfect, but our son was the perfect fit for us.

It's getting easier each day to see God's purposes in our family. Kasi and I are getting a little better at realizing how slow to understand we can be. The perspective gets a little clearer every minute.

But to get to a healthier place, we had to move past the religious jargon and return our focus to the intended truth of the Word of God. We had to dig deeper than the lies of what cultural Christianity had to offer and get real with the Scriptures again. Thankfully, this caused us to get honest about our struggles and become authentically unafraid to speak about our failures and letdowns. Then and only then did we begin to walk in freedom, the sweet freedom that brings beautiful comfort and the transformational power to walk through any storm and face any mountain, because we know that God is doing all things for His glory and our good. It's in this freedom that we realize that *we* are the handicapped ones but that we also serve a God who is patient, kind, and full of healing power.

When that comment was made about "the handicapped one," it shouldn't have been made about my son in a wheelchair. It should have been made about me, before God used that precious little love to wreck me. What might be handicapping you? Before God brought something to life in our family, something else needed to die. What needs to die off in your life so that God can move in you the way He wants to? I pray He will continue to show you every day.

Remember, He won't direct you, transform you, or free you with pithy statements that aren't even true. He will do it with His own power and with the truth of Scripture. Sometimes the most effective way to move forward in freedom is to return to the basics of who God is and to dive deeply into His Word. "The Lord is the Spirit, and where the Spirit of the Lord is, there is freedom" (2 Corinthians 3:17). Freedom can be found where the Spirit is, and what does the Spirit stay close to? That's right—truth. "You will know the truth, and the truth will set you free" (John 8:32). These are the worshippers God is looking for: those who walk in freedom because they walk in spirit and truth. You can't have one without the other. "God is spirit, and those who worship him must worship in spirit and truth" (John 4:24).

I'd Love to Hear from You

If you've found that this book was helpful to you in any way, or if you have any questions, I want to be a help to you. So let's connect!

Facebook—@ShanePruittTX

Twitter/Instagram—@shane_pruitt78

Email—contact@shanepruitt.com (Yes, it's really my personal email, and I'd be honored to hear from you.)

Acknowledgments

Mom and Dad: You have been a constant source of inspiration and encouragement for me. You continue to teach me the value of faithfulness and working hard. Thank you for being an example to Kasi and me of how to have a loving marriage that lasts a lifetime. We are so appreciative of how you love us and your grandbabies.

My wife's family—Tommy and Kelly, Poppy (who is now with Jesus) and Meemaw, and Rex: Thank you for making me part of the family from day one. You have been an ongoing picture of love, grace, and support for our family. Words can't fully describe what you all mean to Kasi, me, and the kiddos.

Dr. Jim Richards: I am so grateful for your leadership and friendship in my life. You are like Paul to me. The Lord uses you to mold and encourage me to be a better father, husband, and follower of Jesus. It's an honor and privilege to serve under your leadership. Thank you for your sacred trust in me to serve our churches in Texas.

Our friends who have become like family to us: You know who you are. Kasi and I constantly thank our great God for surrounding us with such an awesome community of people. Your support to our family is something we deeply, deeply value. We can only pray that we are as much a blessing to you as you have been to us.

Whitney Gossett, John Blase, and Andrew Stoddard: I am forever indebted to you because this book would not be possible without you.

Tony Wolfe and Gabby Brown: Your input on the content was extremely valuable to me.